Laurence Binyon
engraving by William Strang

Emery Walker Ph.x.

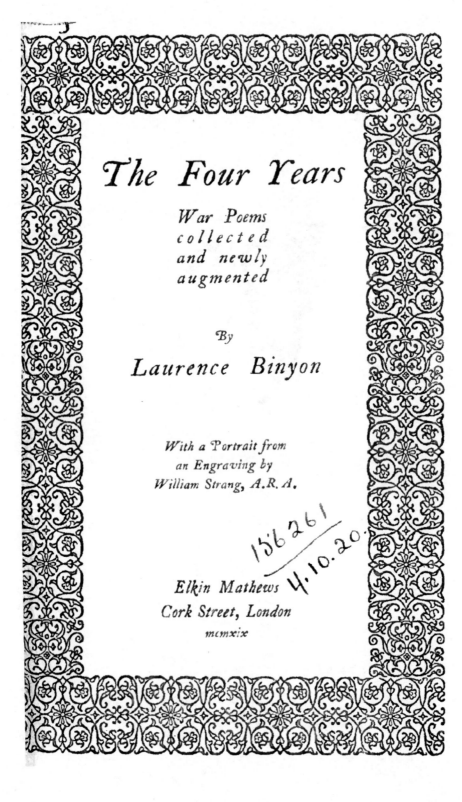

The Four Years

War Poems
collected
and newly
augmented

By

Laurence Binyon

With a Portrait from
an Engraving by
William Strang, A.R.A.

Elkin Mathews
Cork Street, London
mcmxix

Second Edition

DEDICATED TO

RICHARD HENRY POWELL

2ND LIEUT., CINQUE PORTS BATTALION,
ROYAL SUSSEX REGIMENT

IN MEMORY.

STRONG, LOYAL-SOULED, FULL-HEARTED, BLITHELY
  BRAVE,
ONLY REMEMBERING LOVE KNOWS ALL HE GAVE:
BEAUTIFUL BE THE STARS ABOVE HIS GRAVE.

BY THE SAME WRITER

ODES
LONDON VISIONS
THE WINNOWING-FAN
THE ANVIL
THE NEW WORLD

CONTENTS

PRELUDES

B

EUROPE MDCCCCI

TO NAPOLEON

SOARS still thy spirit, Child of Fire?
Dost hear the camps of Europe hum ?
On eagle wings dost hover nigher
At the far rolling of the drum ?
To see the harvest thou hast sown
Smilest thou now, Napoleon ?

Long had the world in blinded mirth
Or suffering patience dreamed content,
When lo ! like thunder over earth
Thy challenge pealed, the skies were rent
Thy terrible youth rose up alone
Against the old world on its throne.

With shuddering then the peoples gazed,
And such a stupor bound them dumb
As those fierce Colchian ranks amazed

EUROPE MDCCCCI

Who saw the youthful Jason come,
And challenging the War-God's name
Step forth, his fiery yoke to tame.

He took those dread bulls by the horn,
Harnessed their fury to his will,
And in the furrow swiftly torn
The dragon's teeth abroad did spill :
Behold, behind his trampling heel
The furrow flowered into steel !

A spear, a plume, a warrior sprung—
Arm'd gods in wrath by hundreds ; he
Faced all, and full amidst them flung
His magic helmet : instantly
Their swords upon themselves they drew,
And shouting each the other slew.

But no Medean spell was thine,
Napoleon, nor anointed charm ;
Thy will was as a fate divine
To wavering men who watched thine arm
Drive on through Europe old thy plough.
The harvest ripens even now !

Time's purple flauntings, king and crown,
Old custom's tall and idle weeds,
Were tossed aside and trampled down,
While thou didst scatter fiery seeds,
That in the gendering lap of earth
Prepared a new world's Titan birth.

Then in thy path from underground,
Where long benumbed in trance they froze,
The Nations, giant forms unbound,
Slow to their aching stature rose ;
And through their wintry veins again
Slow flushed the streams of life in pain.

Thy thunder, O Napoleon, passed,
But these whom thou hadst stirred to life,
On them the imperious doom was cast
Of inextinguishable strife.
For peace they long, but blood and tears
Still blinded the tempestuous years.

A hundred years have flown, and still
For peace they pine ; peace tarries yet.
These groaning armies Europe fill,

And war's red planet hath not set.
O mockery of peace, that gnaws
Their hearts for so abhorred a cause!

Is peace so easy ?   Nay, the names
That are most dear and most divine
To men, are like the heavenly flames
That farthest from possession shine.
Peace, love, truth, freedom, unto these
The way is through the storming seas.

Ye wakened Nations, now no more
You battle for a monarch's whim ;
The cause is now in your heart's core,
Your soul must strive through every limb ;
They who with all their soul contend
Bear more, but to a nobler end.

Be patient in your strife ! And thou,
O England, dearer than the rest ;
England, with proud looks on thy brow,
England, with trouble at thy breast,
Seek on in patient fortitude
Strong peace, most worthy to be wooed.

Take up thy task, O nobly born !
With both hands grasp thy destiny.
Easy is ignorance, easy scorn,
And fluent pride, unworthy thee.
Grand rolls the planet of thy fate :
Be thy just passions also great !

Turn from the sweet lure of content,
Rise up among the courts of ease ;
Be all thy will as a bow bent,
Thy sure oncoming like thy seas.
Purge clear within thy deep desires
To be our burning altar-fires !

Then welcome peril, so it bring
Thy true soul leaping into light ;
A glory for our mouths to sing
And for our deeds to match in might,
Till thou at last our hope enthrone
And make indeed thy peace our own.

JANUARY, 1901.

THE BELFRY OF BRUGES

KEEN comes the dizzy air
In one tumultuous breath.
The tower to heaven lies bare ;
Dumb stir the streets beneath.

Immeasurable sky
Domes upward from the dim
Round land, the astonished eye
Supposes the world's rim.

And through the sea of space
Winds drive the furious cloud
Silent in endless race ;
And the tower rocks aloud.

Mine eye now wanders wide,
My thought now quickens keen.
O cities, far descried,
What ravage have you seen

Of an enkindled world ? ·
Homes blazing and hearths bare ;
Of hosts tyrannic hurled
On pale ranks of despair,

Who fed with warm proud blood
The cause unquenchable,
For which your heroes stood,
For which our Sidney fell ;

Sidney, whose starry fame,
Mirrored in noble song,
Shines, all our sloth to shame,
And arms us against wrong ;

Bright star, that seems to burn
Over yon English shore,
Whither my feet return,
And my thoughts run before ;

Run with this rumour brought
By the wild wind's alarms,
Dark sounds with battle fraught,
Menace of distant arms.

O menace harsh, but vain !
For what can peril do
But search our souls again
To sift and find the true ?

Prove if the sap of old
Shoots yet from the old seed,
If faith be still unsold,
If truth be truth indeed?

Welcome the blast that shakes
The wall wherein we have lain
Slumbering, our heart awakes
And rends the prison chain.

Turn we from prosperous toys
And the dull name of ease ;
Rather than tarnished joys
Face we the angry seas !

Or if old age infirm
Be in our veins congealed,
Bow we to Time, our term
Fulfilled, and proudly yield.

Not each to each we are made,
Not each to each we fall,
But every true part played
Quickens the heart of all

That feeds and moves and fires
The many-peopled lands,
And in our languor tires,
But in our strength expands.

For forward-gazing eyes
Fate shall no terror keep.
She in our own breast lies :
Now let her wake from sleep !

1898.

THUNDER ON THE DOWNS

WIDE earth, wide heaven, and in the summer
  air
Silence ! The summit of the down is bare
Between the climbing crests of wood ; but
  those
Great sea-winds, wont, when the wet South-West
  blows,
To rock tall beeches and strong oaks aloud
And strew torn leaves upon the streaming cloud
To-day are idle, slumbering far aloof.
Under the solemn height and gorgeous roof
Of cloud-built sky, all earth is indolent.
Wandering hum of bees and thymy scent
Of the short turf enrich pure loneliness :
Scarcely an airy topmost-twining tress
Of bryony quivers where the thorn it wreathes ;
Hot fragrance from the honeysuckle breathes ;
And sweet the rose floats on the arching briar's
Green fountain, sprayed with delicate frail fires.
For clumps of thicket, dark beneath the blaze
Of the high westering sun, beset the ways

Of smooth grass, narrowing where the slope runs
  steep
Down to green woods, and glowing shadows keep
A freshness round the mossy roots, and cool
The light that sleeps as in a chequered pool
Of golden air. O woods, I love you well,
I love the flowers you hide, your ferny smell ;
But here is sweeter solitude, for here
My heart breathes heavenly space ; the sky is
  near
To thought, with heights that fathomlessly
  glow ;
And the eye wanders the wide land below.

And this is England ! June's undarkened green
Gleams on far woods ; and in the vales between
Grey hamlets, older than the trees that shade
Their ripening meadows, are in quiet laid,
Themselves a part of the warm, fruitful ground.
The little hills of England rise around ;
The little streams that wander from them shine
And with their names remembered names en-
  twine
Of old renown and honour, fields of blood
High causes fought on, stubborn hardihood
For freedom spent, and songs, our noblest pride,

That in the heart of England never died
And, burning still, make splendour of our tongue.
Glories enacted, spoken, suffered, sung !
You lie emblazoned on this land now sleeping ;
And southward, over leagues of forest sweeping,
White on the verge glistens the famous sea,
That English wave, on which so haughtily
Towered her sails, and one sail homeward bore
Past capes of silently lamenting shore
Victory's dearest dead. O shores of home,
Since by the vanished watch-fire shields of Rome
Dinted this upland turf, what hearts have ached
To see you far away, what eyes have waked
Ere dawn to watch those cliffs of long desire
One after one rise in their voiceless choir
Out of the twilight over the rough blue
Like music ! . . .
              But now heavy gleams imbrue
The inland air. Breathless the valleys hold
Their colours in a veil of sultry gold
With mingled shadows that have ceased to
    crawl ;
For far in heaven is thunder ! Over all
A single cloud in slow magnificence
Climbs like a mountain, gradual and immense
With awful head unstirring, and moved on

Against the zenith, towers above the sun.
And still it thickens luminous fold on fold
Of fatal colour, ominously scrolled
And fleeced with fire ; above the sun it towers
Like some vast thought quickening a world not
   ours
Remote in the waste blue, as if behind
Its rim were splendour that could smite us blind,
So doom-piled and intense it crests heaven's
  height
And mounting makes a menace of the light.

A menace ! Yes, for when light comes, we fear.
Light, that may touch, as the pure angel-spear,
Us to ourselves, make visible, make start
The apparition of the very heart
And mystery of our thoughts, awaked from under
The mask of cheating habit, and to thunder
Bare in a moment of white fire what we
Have feared and fled, our own reality.

And if a lightning now were loosed in flame
Out of the darkness of the cloud to claim
Thy heart, O England, how wouldst thou be
   known
In that hour ? How to the quick core be shown

And seen ?   What cry should from thy very soul
Answer the judgment of that thunder-roll ?

I hear a voice arraign thee.   " Where is now
The exaltation that once lit thy brow ?
Thou countest all thy ocean-sundered lands.
Thou heapest up the labours of thy hands,
Thou seest all thy ships upon the seas.
But in thy own heart mean idolatries
Usurp devotion, choke thee and annul
Noble excess of spirit, and make dull
Thine eyes, enfleshed with much dominion.
Art thou so great and is the glory gone ?
Do these bespeak thy freedom who deflower
Time, and make barren every senseless hour,
Who from themselves hurry, like men afraid
Lest what they are be to themselves betrayed ?
Or those who in their huddled thousands sweat
To buy the sleep that helps them to forget ?—
Life lies unused, life in its loveliness !
While the cry ravens still, ' Possess, Possess ! '
And there is no possession.   All the lust
Of gainful man is quieted in dust ;
His faith, his fear, his joy, his doom he owns,
No more ; the rest is parcelled with his bones,
Save what the imagination of his heart

Can to the labour of his hands impart,
Making stones serve his spirit's desire, and
  breathe.
But thou, what dost thou to the world bequeath,
Who gatherest riches in a waste of mind
Into what end, O confidently blind,
Forgetful of the things that grow not old
And alone live and are not bought or sold ! "

Speaks that voice truth ? Is it for this that great
And tender spirits suffered scorn and hate,
Loved to the utmost, poured themselves, gave all
Nor counted lost, spirits imperial ?
Where are they now, they that our memory
  guard
Among the nations ? Shall I say, enstarred
And throned aloof ? No, not from heavens of
  thought
Watching our muddied brief procession, not
Judges sublime above us, without share
In our thronged ways of struggle, hope, despair,
But in our blood, our dreams, our deeds they stir,
Strive on our lips for language, shame and spur
The sluggard in us, out of darkness come
Like summoned champions when the world is
  dumb.

  C

Within our hearts they wait with all they gave.
Woe to us, woe, if we become their grave !
It shall not be. Darken thy pall, and trail,
Thunder of heaven, above the valleys pale !
Another England in my vision glows.
And she is armed within ; at last she knows
Herself, and what to her own soul belongs.
Mid the world's irremediable wrongs
She keeps her faith ; and nothing of her name
Or of her handiwork but doth proclaim
Her purpose. Her own soul hath made her
    free,
Not circumstance ; she knows no victory
Save of the mind : in her is nothing done,
No wrong, no shame, no glory of any one,
But is the cause of all and each, a thing
Felt like a fire to kindle and to sting
The proud blood of a nation. On her brows
Is hope ; her body doth her spirit house
Express and eloquent, not numb and frore ;
And her voice echoes over sea and shore,
And all the lands and isles that are her own
In choric interchange and antiphon
Answer, as fancy hears in yonder cloud
From vale to vale repeated low and loud
The still suspended thunder.

Hearts of Youth,
High-beating, ardent, quick in hope and ruth
And noble anger, O wherever now
You dedicate your uncorrupted vow
To be an energy of Light, a sword
Of the ever-living Will, amid abhorred
Din of the reeking street and populous den
Where under the great stars blind lusts of men
War on each other, or escaped to hills
Where peace the solitary evening fills,
Or far remote on other soils of earth
Keeping the dearness of your fathers' hearth
On vast plains of the West, or Austral strands
Of the warm underworld, or storied lands
Of the orient sun, or over ocean ways
Stemming the wave through blue or stormy
    days
Wherever, as the circling light slopes round,
On human lips is heard an English sound,
O scattered, silent, hidden and unknown,
Be lifted up, for you are not alone !
High-beating hearts, to your deep vows be true !
Live out your dreams, for England lives in you.

MIDSUMMER, 1911.

THE WINNOWING FAN

THE FOURTH OF AUGUST

Now in thy splendour go before us,
Spirit of England, ardent-eyed,
Enkindle this dear earth that bore us,
In the hour of peril purified.

The cares we hugged drop out of vision,
Our hearts with deeper thoughts dilate.
We step from days of sour division
Into the grandeur of our fate.

For us the glorious dead have striven,
They battled that we might be free.
We to their living cause are given;
We arm for men that are to be.

Among the nations nobliest chartered,
England recalls her heritage.
In her is that which is not bartered,
Which force can neither quell nor cage.

23

For her immortal stars are burning ;
With her the hope that's never done,
The seed that's in the Spring's returning,
The very flower that seeks the sun.

She fights the fraud that feeds desire on
Lies, in a lust to enslave or kill,
The barren creed of blood and iron,
Vampire of Europe's wasted will . . .

Endure, O Earth ! and thou, awaken,
Purged by this dreadful winnowing-fan,
O wronged, untameable, unshaken
Soul of divinely suffering man.

STRANGE FRUIT

THIS year the grain is heavy-ripe ;
The apple shows a ruddier stripe ;
Never berries so profuse
Blackened with so sweet a juice
On brambly hedges, summer-dyed.
The yellow leaves begin to glide ;
But Earth in careless lap-ful treasures
Pledge of over-brimming measures,
As if some rich unwonted zest
Stirred prodigal within her breast.
And now, while plenty's left uncared,
The fruit unplucked, the sickle spared,
Where men go forth to waste and spill,
Toiling to burn, destroy, and kill,
Lo, also side by side with these
Beast-hungers, ravening miseries,
The heart of man has brought to birth
Splendours richer than his earth.
Now in the thunder-hour of fate
Each one is kinder to his mate ;
The surly smile ; the hard forbear ;
There's help and hope for all to share ;

And sudden visions of goodwill
Transcending all the scope of ill
Like a glory of rare weather
Link us in common light together,
A clearness of the cleansing sun,
Where none's alone and all are one ;
And touching each a priceless pain
We find our own true hearts again.
No more the easy masks deceive :
We give, we dare, and we believe.

THE NEW IDOL

MAGNIFICENT the Beast! Look in the eyes
Of the fell tiger towering on his prey,
Beautiful in his power to pounce and slay
And effortless in action. He denies
All but himself. He gloats on his weak prize,
Roaring the anger of wild breath at bay,
Blank anger like an element whose way
Is mere annihilation! Terrible eyes!

But there is one more to be feared, who can
Escape the prison of his own wrath; whose will
Lives beyond life; who smiles with quiet lips;
Most terrible because most tender, Man,—
Not only uncowed but irresistible
When the cause fires him to the finger-tips.

THE HARVEST

RED reapers under these sad August skies,
Proud War-Lords, careless of ten thousand dead,
Who leave earth's kindly crops unharvested
As you have left the kindness of the wise
For brutal menace and for clumsy lies,
The spawn of insolence by bragging fed,
With power and fraud in faith's and honour's
   stead,
Accounting these but good stupidities ;

You reap a heavier harvest than you know.
Disnaturing a nation, you have thieved
Her name, her patient genius, while you thought
To fool the world and master it. You sought
Reality. It comes in hate and woe.
In the end you also shall not be deceived.

TO THE BELGIANS

O RACE that Cæsar knew,
That won stern Roman praise,
What land not envies you
The laurel of these days ?

You built your cities rich
Around each towered hall,—
Without, the statued niche,
Within, the pictured wall.

Your ship-thronged wharves, your marts
With gorgeous Venice vied.
Peace and her famous arts
Were yours : though tide on tide

Of Europe's battle scourged
Black field and reddened soil,
From blood and smoke emerged
Peace and her fruitful toil.

Yet when the challenge rang,
"The War-Lord comes; give room!"
Fearless to arms you sprang
Against the odds of doom.

Like your own Damian
Who sought that lepers' isle
To die a simple man
For men with tranquil smile,

So strong in faith you dared
Defy the giant, scorn
Ignobly to be spared,
Though trampled, spoiled, and torn,

And in your faith arose
And smote, and smote again,
Till those astonished foes
Reeled from their mounds of slain;

The faith that the free soul,
Untaught by force to quail,
Through fire and dirge and dole
Prevails and shall prevail.

Still for your frontier stands
The host that knew no dread,
Your little, stubborn land's
Nameless, immortal dead.

LOUVAIN

To Dom Bruno Destrée, O.S.B.

I

It was the very heart of Peace that thrilled
In the deep minster-bell's wide-throbbing sound
When over old roofs evening seemed to build
Security this world has never found.

Your cloister looked from Cæsar's rampart, high
O'er the fair city : clustered orchard-trees
Married their murmur with the dreaming sky.
It was the house of lore and living peace.

And there we talked of youth's delightful years
In Italy, in England. Now, O Friend,
I know not if I speak to living ears
Or if upon you too is come the end.

Peace is on Louvain ; dead peace of spilt blood
Upon the mounded ashes where she stood.

II

But from that blood, those ashes, there arose
Not hoped-for terror cowering as it ran,
But divine anger flaming upon those
Defamers of the very name of man,

Abortions of their blind hyena-creed,
Who for " protection " of their battle-host
Against the unarmed of them they had made to
   bleed,
Whose hearts they had tortured to the utter-
   most

Without a cause, past pardon, fired and tore
The towers of fame and beauty, while they shot
And butchered the defenceless in the door.
But History shall hang them high, to rot

Unburied, in the face of times unborn,
Mankind's abomination and last scorn.

TO GOETHE

GOETHE, who saw and who foretold
   A world revealed
New-springing from its ashes old
   On Valmy field,

When Prussia's sullen hosts retired
   Before the advance
Of ragged, starved, but freedom-fired
   Soldiers of France ;

If still those clear, Olympian eyes
   Through smoke and rage
Your ancient Europe scrutinize,
   What think you, Sage ?

Are these the armies of the Light
   That seek to drown
The light of lands where freedom's fight
   Has won renown ?

Will they blot also out your name
   Because you praise
All works of men that shrine the flame
   Of beauty's ways,

Wherever men have proved them great,
   Nor, drunk with pride,
Saw but a single swollen State
   And naught beside,

Nor dreamed of drilling Europe's mind
   With threat and blow
The way professors have designed
   Genius should go ?

Or shall a people rise at length
   And see, and shake
The fetters from its giant strength,
   And grandly break

This pedantry of feud and force
   To man untrue
Thundering and blundering on its course
   To death and rue ?

AT RHEIMS

THEIR hearts were burning in their breasts
   Too hot for curse or cries.
They stared upon the towers that burned
   Before their smarting eyes.

There where, since France began to be,
   Anointed kings knelt down,
There where the Maid, the unafraid,
   Received her vision's crown,

The senseless shell with nightmare scream
   Burst, and fair fragments fell
Torn from their centuries of peace
   As by the rage of hell.

What help for wrath, what use for wail ?
   Before a dumb despair
All ancient, high, heroic France
   Seemed burning, bleeding there.

     .   .   .   .   .

Within, the pillars soar to gloom
  Lit by the glimmering Rose ;
Spirits of beauty shrined in stone
  Afar from mortal woes,

Hearing not, though their haunted shade
  Is stricken, and all around
With splintering flash and brutal crash
  The ghostly aisles resound.

And there, upon the pavement stretched,
  The German wounded groan
To see the dropping flames of death
  And feel the shells their own.

Too fierce the fire ! Helped by their foes
  They stagger out to air..
The green-gray coats are seen, are known
  Through all the crowded square.

.   .   .   .   .

Ah, now for vengeance ! Deep the groan :
  A death-knell ! Quietly
Soldiers unsling their rifles, lift
  And aim with steady eye.

But sudden in the hush between
  Death and the doomed, there stands
Against those levelled guns a priest,
  Gentle, with outstretched hands.

Be not as guilty as they! he cries . . .
  Each lets his weapon fall,
As if a vision showed him France
  And vengeance vain and small.

TO THE ENEMY COMPLAINING

BE ruthless, then ; scorn slaves of scruple ; avow
The blow, planned with such patience, that you
  deal
So terribly ; hack on, and care not how
The innocent fall ; live out your faith of steel.

Then you speak speech that we can comprehend.
It cries from the unpitied blood you spill.
And so we stand against you, and to the end
Flame as one man, the weapon of one will.

But when your lips usurp the loyal phrase
Of honour, querulously voluble
Of " chivalry " and " kindness," and you praise
What you despise for weakness of the fool,

Then the gorge rises. Bleat to dupe the dead !
The wolf beneath the sheepskin drips too red.

TO WOMEN

YOUR hearts are lifted up, your hearts
That have foreknown the utter price.
Your hearts burn upward like a flame
Of splendour and of sacrifice.

For you, you too, to battle go,
Not with the marching drums and cheers
But in the watch of solitude
And through the boundless night of fears.

Swift, swifter than those hawks of war,
Those threatening wings that pulse the air,
Far as the vanward ranks are set,
You are gone before them, you are there!

And not a shot comes blind with death
And not a stab of steel is pressed
Home, but invisibly it tore
And entered first a woman's breast.

Amid the thunder of the guns,
The lightnings of the lance and sword,
Your hope, your dread, your throbbing pride,
Your infinite passion is outpoured

From hearts that are as one high heart
Withholding naught from doom and bale,
Burningly offered up,—to bleed,
To bear, to break, but not to fail!

FOR THE FALLEN

WITH proud thanksgiving, a mother for her
   children,
England mourns for her dead across the sea.
Flesh of her flesh they were, spirit of her
   spirit,
Fallen in the cause of the free.

Solemn the drums thrill: Death august and
   royal
Sings sorrow up into immortal spheres.
There is music in the midst of desolation
And a glory that shines upon our tears.

They went with songs to the battle, they were
   young,
Straight of limb, true of eye, steady and
   aglow.
They were staunch to the end against odds
   uncounted,
They fell with their faces to the foe.

They shall grow not old, as we that are left grow
    old :
Age shall not weary them, nor the years con-
    demn.
At the going down of the sun and in the morning
We will remember them.

They mingle not with their laughing comrades
    again ;
They sit no more at familiar tables of home ;
They have no lot in our labour of the day-time ;
They sleep beyond England's foam.

But where our desires are and our hopes pro-
    found,
Felt as a well-spring that is hidden from sight,
To the innermost heart of their own land they
    are known
As the stars are known to the Night ;

As the stars that shall be bright when we are
    dust,
Moving in marches upon the heavenly plain,
As the stars that are starry in the time of our
    darkness,
To the end, to the end, they remain.

ODE FOR SEPTEMBER

I

On that long day when England held her breath,
Suddenly gripped at heart
And called to choose her part
Between her loyal soul and luring sophistries,
We watched the wide, green-bosomed land
    beneath
Driven and tumultuous skies ;
We watched the volley of white shower after
    shower
Desolate with fierce drops the fallen flower ;
And still the rain's retreat
Drew glory on its track,
And still, when all was darkness and defeat,
Upon dissolving cloud the bow of peace shone
    back.
So in our hearts was alternating beat,
With very dread elate ;
And Earth dyed all her day in colours of our
    fate.

II

But oh, how faint the image we foretold
In fancies of our fear
Now that the truth is here !
And we awake from dream yet think it still a
dream.
It bursts our thoughts with more than thought
can hold ;
And more than human seem
These agonies of conflict ; Elements
At war ! yet not with vast indifference
Casually crushing ; nay,
It is as if were hurled
Lightnings that murdered, seeking out their
prey ;
As if an earthquake shook to chaos half the
world,
Equal in purpose as in power to slay ;
And thunder stunned our ears
Streaming in rain of blood on torrents that are
tears.

III

Around a planet rolls the drum's alarm.
Far where the summer smiles
Upon the utmost isles,
Danger is treading silent as a fever-breath.
Now in the North the secret waters arm ;
Under the wave is Death :
They fight in the very air, the virgin air,
Hovering on fierce wings to the onset : there
Nations to battle stream ;
Earth smokes and cities burn ;
Heaven thickens in a storm of shells that scream;
The long lines shattering break, turn and again
    return ;
And still across a continent they teem,
Moving in myriads ; more
Than ranks of flesh and blood, but soul with
    soul at war !

IV

All the hells are awake : the old serpents hiss
From dungeons of the mind ;
Fury of hate born blind,
Madness and lust, despairs and treacheries un-
    clean ;
They shudder up from man's most dark abyss.
But there are heavens serene
That answer strength with strength ; they
    stand secure ;
They arm us from within, and we endure.
Now are the brave more brave,
Now is the cause more dear,
The more the tempests of the darkness rave,
As, when the sun goes down, the shining stars
    are clear.
Radiant the spirit rushes to the grave.
Glorious it is to live
In such an hour, but life is lovelier yet to give.

V

Alas ! what comfort for the uncomforted,
Who knew no cause, nor sought
Glory or gain ? they are taught,
Homeless in homes that burn, what human
    hearts can bear.
The children stumble over their dear dead,
Wandering they know not where.
And there is one who simply fights, obeys,
Tramps, till he loses count of nights and days,
Tired, mired in dust and sweat,
Far from his own hearth-stone ;
A common man of common earth, and yet
The battle-winner he, a man of no renown,
Where " food for cannon " pays a nation's
    debt.
This is Earth's hero, whom
The pride of Empire tosses careless to his
    doom

VI

Now will we speak, while we have eyes for tears
And fibres to be wrung
And in our mouths a tongue.
We will bear wrongs untold but will not only
    bear ;
Not only bear, but build through striving years
The answer of our prayer,
That whatsoever has the noble name
Of man, shall not be yoked to alien shame ;
That life shall be indeed
Life, not permitted breath
Of spirits wrenched and forced to others' need,
Robbed of their nature's joy and free alone in
    death.
The world shall travail in that cause, shall bleed,
But deep in hope it dwells
Until the morning break which the long night
    foretells.

E

VII

O children filled with your own airy glee
Or with a grief that comes
So swift, so strange, it numbs,
If on your growing youth this page of terror bite,
Harden not then your senses, feel and be
The promise of the light.
O heirs of Man, keep in your hearts not less
The divine torrents of his tenderness !
'Tis ever war : but rust
Grows on the sword ; the tale
Of earth is strewn with empires heaped in dust
Because they dreamed that force should punish
      and prevail.
The will to kindness lives beyond their lust ;
Their grandeurs are undone :
Deep, deep within man's soul are all his vic-
      tories won.

THE ANVIL

THE ANVIL

BURNED from the ore's rejected dross
The iron whitens in the heat.
With plangent strokes of pain and loss
The hammers on the iron beat.
Searched by the fire, through death and dole
We feel the iron in our soul.

O dreadful Forge ! if torn and bruised
The heart, more urgent comes our cry
Not to be spared but to be used,
Brain, sinew, and spirit, before we die.
Beat out the iron, edge it keen,
And shape us to the end we mean !

THE HEALERS

In a vision of the night I saw them,
    In the battles of the night.
'Mid the roar and the reeling shadows of blood
    They were moving like light,

Light of the reason, guarded
    Tense within the will,
As a lantern under a tossing of boughs
    Burns steady and still.

With scrutiny calm, and with fingers
    Patient as swift
They bind up the hurts and the pain-writhen
    Bodies uplift,

Untired and defenceless; around them
    With shrieks in its breath
Bursts stark from the terrible horizon
    Impersonal death;

But they take not their courage from anger
  That blinds the hot being ;
They take not their pity from weakness ;
  Tender, yet seeing ;

Feeling, yet nerved to the uttermost ;
  Keen, like steel ;
Yet the wounds of the mind they are stricken
      with,
  Who shall heal ?

They endure to have eyes of the watcher
  In hell, and not swerve
For an hour from the faith that they follow,
  The light that they serve.

Man true to man, to his kindness
  That overflows all,
To his spirit erect in the thunder
  When all his forts fall,—

This light, in the tiger-mad welter
  They serve and they save.
What song shall be worthy to sing of them—
  Braver than the brave ?

THE ZEPPELIN

GUNS! far and near,
Quick, sudden, angry,
They startle the still street.
Upturned faces appear,
Doors open on darkness,
There is a hurrying of feet,

And whirled athwart gloom
White fingers of alarm
Point at last there
Where illumined and dumb
A shape suspended
Hovers, a demon of the starry air!

Strange and cold as a dream
Of sinister fancy,
It charms like a snake,
Poised deadly in a gleam,
While bright explosions
Leap up to it and break,

Is it terror you seek
To exult in ?   Know then
Hearts are here
That the plunging beak
Of night-winged murder
Strikes not with fear

So much as it strings
To a deep elation
And a quivering pride
That at last the hour brings
For them too the danger
Of those who died,

Of those who yet fight
Spending for each of us
Their glorious blood
In the foreign night,—
That now we are neared to them
Thank we God.

ORPHANS OF FLANDERS

WHERE is the land that fathered, nourished, poured
The sap of a strong race into your veins,
Land of wide tilth, of farms and granaries stored,
Of old towers chiming over peaceful plains ?

It is become a vision, barred away
Like light in cloud, a memory and belief.
On those lost plains the Glory of yesterday
Builds her dark towers for the bells of Grief.

It is become a splendour-circled name
For all the world ; a torch against the skies
Burns on that blood-spot, the unpardoned shame
Of them that conquered : but your homeless
eyes

See rather some brown pond by a white wall,
Red cattle crowding in the rutty lane,
A garden, where the hollyhocks were tall
In the Augusts that shall never be again.

There your thoughts cling as the long-thrusting
    root
Clings in the ground ; your orphaned hearts are
    there.
O mates of sunburnt earth, your love is mute
But strong like thirst and deeper than despair.

You have endured what pity can but grope
To feel : into that darkness enters none.
We have but hands to help ; yours is the hope
Whose courage rises silent with the sun.

THE ENGLISH GRAVES

THE rains of yesterday are flown,
And light is on the farthest hills ;
The homeliest rough grass by the stone
To radiance thrills ;

And the wet bank above the ditch,
Trailing its thorny bramble, shows
Soft apparitions, clustered rich,
Of the pure primrose.

The shining stillness breathes, vibrates
From simple earth to lonely sky,
A hinted wonder that awaits
The heart's reply.

O lovely life ! the chaffinch sings
High on the hazel, near and clear.
Sharp to the heart's blood, sweetness springs
In the morning here.

But my heart goes with the young cloud
That voyages the April light
Southward, across the beaches loud
And cliffs of white

To fields of France, far fields that spread
Beyond the tumbling of the waves,
And touches as with shadowy tread
The English graves.

There too is Earth that never weeps,
The unrepining Earth, that holds
The secret of a thousand sleeps
And there unfolds

Flowers of sweet ignorance on the slope
Where strong arms dropped and blood choked
    breath,
Earth that forgets all things but hope
And smiles on death.

They poured their spirits out in pride,
They throbbed away the price of years:
Now that dear ground is glorified
With dreams, with tears.

THE ENGLISH GRAVES

A flower there is sown, to bud
And bloom beyond our loss and smart:
Noble France, at its root is blood
From England's heart.

FETCHING THE WOUNDED

At the road's end glimmer the station lights ;
How small beneath the immense hollow of
  Night's
Lonely and living silence ! Air that raced
And tingled on the eyelids as we faced
The long road stretched between the poplars
  flying
To the dark behind us, shuddering and sighing
With phantom foliage, lapses into hush.
Magical supersession ! The loud rush
Swims into quiet ; midnight reassumes
Its solitude ; there's nothing but great glooms,
Blurred stars ; whispering gusts ; the hum of
  wires.
And swerving leftwards upon noiseless tires
We glide over the grass that smells of dew.
A wave of wonder bathes my body through !
For there in the headlamps' gloom-surrounded
  beam
Tall flowers spring before us, like a dream,
Each luminous little green leaf intimate

And motionless, distinct and delicate
With powdery white bloom fresh upon the stem,
As if that clear beam had created them
Out of the darkness.   Never so intense
I felt the pang of beauty's innocence,
Earthly and yet unearthly.

                              A sudden call !
We leap to ground, and I forget it all.
Each hurries on his errand ; lanterns swing ;
Dark shapes cross and re-cross the rails ; we
      bring
Stretchers, and pile and number them ; and
      heap
The blankets ready.   Then we wait and keep
A listening ear.   Nothing comes yet ; all's still.
Only soft gusts upon the wires blow shrill
Fitfully, with a gentle spot of rain.
Then, ere one knows it, the long gradual train
Creeps quietly in and slowly stops.   No sound
But a few voices' interchange.   Around
Is the immense night-stillness, the expanse
Of faint stars over all the wounds of France.

Now stale odour of blood mingles with keen
Pure smell of grass and dew.   Now lantern sheen
Falls on brown faces opening patient eyes

And lips of gentle answers, where each lies
Supine upon his stretcher, black of beard
Or with young cheeks ; on cap and tunic
    smeared
And stained, white bandages round foot or head
Or arm, discoloured here and there with red.
Sons of all corners of wide France ; from Lille,
Douay, the land beneath the invader's heel,
Champagne, Touraine, the fisher-villages
Of Brittany, the valleyed Pyrenees,
Blue coasts of the South, old Paris streets.
    Argonne
Of ever smouldering battle, that anon
Leaps furious, brothered them in arms. They
    fell
In the trenched forest scarred with reeking shell.
Now strange the sound comes round them in the
    night
Of English voices. By the wavering light
Quickly we have borne them, one by one, to the
    air,
And sweating in the dark lift up with care,
Tense-sinewed, each to his place. The cars at
    last
Complete their burden : slowly, and then fast
We glide away.

F

And the dim round of sky,
Infinite and silent, broods unseeingly
Over the shadowy uplands rolling black
Into far woods, and the long road we track
Bordered with apparitions, as we pass,
Of trembling poplars and lamp-whitened grass,
A brief procession flitting like a thought
Through a brain drowsing into slumber ; nought
But we awake in the solitude immense !
But hurting the vague dumbness of my sense
Are fancies wandering the night : there steals
Into my heart, like something that one feels
In darkness, the still presence of far homes
Lost in deep country, and in little rooms
The vacant bed. I touch the world of pain
That is so silent. Then I see again
Only those infinitely patient faces
In the lantern beam, beneath the night's vast
   spaces,
Amid the shadows and the scented dew ;
And those illumined flowers, springing anew
In freshness like a smile of secrecy
From the gloom-buried earth, return to mc.
The village sleeps ; blank walls, and windows
   barred.
But lights are moving in the hushed courtyard

As we glide up to the open door.   The Chief
Gives every man his order, prompt and brief.
We carry up our wounded, one by one.
The first cock crows : the morrow is begun.

THE EBB OF WAR

In the seven-times taken and retaken town
Peace ! The mind stops ; sense argues against
  sense.
The August sun is ghostly in the street
As if the Silence of a thousand years
Were its familiar. All is as it was
At the instant of the shattering : flat-thrown
  walls ;
Dislocated rafters ; lintels blown awry
And toppling over ; what were windows, mere
Gapings on mounds of dust and shapelessness ;
Charred posts caught in a bramble of twisted
  iron ;
Wires sagging tangled across the street ; the black
Skeleton of a vine, wrenched from the old house
It clung to ; a limp bell-pull ; here and there
Little printed papers pasted on the wall.
It is like a madness crumpled up in stone,
Laughterless, tearless, meaningless ; a frenzy
Stilled, like at ebb the shingle in sea-caves
Where the imagined weight of water swung

Its senseless crash with pebbles in myriads
    churned
By the random seethe. But here was flesh and
    blood,
Seeing eyes, feeling nerves ; memoried minds
With the habit of the picture of these fields
And the white roads crossing the wide green
    plain.
All vanished ! One could fancy the very fields
Were memory's projection, phantoms ! All
Silent ! The stone is hot to the touching hand.
Footsteps come strange to the sense. In the
    sloped churchyard,
Where the tower shows the blue through its
    great rents,
Shadow falls over pitiful wrecked graves,
And on the gravel a bare-headed boy,
Hands in his pockets, with brown absent eyes,
Whistles the Marseillaise : To Arms, To Arms !
There is no other sound in the bright air.
It is as if they heard under the grass,
The dead men of the Marne, and their thin voice
Used those young lips to sing it from their graves,
The song that sang a nation into arms.
And far away to the listening ear in the silence
Like remote thunder throb the guns of France.

THE ANTAGONISTS

I

CAVERNS mouthed with blackness more than
   night,
Bog and jungle deep in strangling brier,
Venom-breeding slime that loathest light,
Who has plumbed your secret ? who the blind
   desire
Hissing from the viper's lifted jaws,
Maddening the beast with scent of prey
Tracked through savage glooms on robber paws
Till the slaughter gluts him red and reeking ?
   Nay,
Man, this breathing mystery, this intense
Body beautiful with thinking eyes,
Master of the spirit outsoaring sense,
Spirit of tears and laughter, who has measured
   all the skies,—
Is he also the lair
Of a lust, of a sting
That hides from the air

Yet is lurking to spring
From the nescient core
Of his fibre, alert
At the trumpet of war
And hungry to hurt,
When he hears from abysses of time
Aboriginal mutters, replying
To something he knew not within him,
And the Demon of Earth crying:

" I am the will of the fire
That bursts into boundless fury ;
I am my own implacable desire.

I am the will of the sea
That shoulders the ships and breaks them ;
There is none other but me."

Heavy forests bred them,
The race that dreamed.
In the bones of savage earth
Their dreams had birth :
Darkness fed them.
And the full brain grossly teemed
With thoughts compressed, with rages
Obstinate, stark, obscure—

Thirsts no time assuages,
But centuries immure.
As the sap of trees, behind
Crumpled bark of bossy boles,
Presses up its juices blind,
Buried within their souls
The dream insatiate still
Nursed its fierceness old
And violent will,
Haunted with twiilght where the Gods drink full
Ere they renew their revelry of slaying,
And warriors leap like the lion on the bull,
And harsh horns in the northern mist are bray-
    ing.
Tenebrous in them lay the dream
Like a fire that under ashes
Smoulders heavy-heaped and dim
Yet with spurted stealthy flashes
Sends a goblin shadow floating
Crooked on the rafters—then
Sudden from its den
Springs in splendour. So should burst
Destiny from dream, from thirst
Rapture gloating
On a vision of earth afar
Stretched for a prize and a prey ;

And the secular might of the Gods re-risen
Savage and glorious, waiting its day,
Should shatter its ancient prison
And leap like the panther to slay,
Magnificent ! Storm, then, and thunder
The haughty to crush with the tame,
For the world is the strong man's plunder
Whose coming is swifter than flame ;
And the nations unready, decayed,
Unworthy of fate or afraid,
Shall be stricken and torn asunder
Or yield in shame.

The Dream is fulfilled.
Is it this that you willed,
O patient ones ?
For this that you gave
Young to the grave
Your valiant sons ?
For this that you wore
Brave faces, and bore
The burden heart-breaking—
Sublimely deceived,
You that bled and believed—
For the Dream ? or the Waking ?

II

No drum-beat, pulsing challenge and desire,
Sounded, no jubilant boast nor fierce alarm
Cried throbbing from enfevered throats afire
For glory, when from vineyard, forge, and farm,
From wharf and warehouse, foundry, shop, and
   school,
From the unreaped cornfield and the office-stool
France called her sons ; but loth, but grave,
But silent, with their purpose proud and hard
Within them, as of men that go to guard
More than life, yet to dare
More than death : France, it was their France
   to save !
Nor now the fiery legend of old fames
And that imperial Eagle whose wide wings
Hovered from Vistula to Finistère,
Who plucked the crown from Kings,
Filled her ; but France was arming in her mind :
The world unborn and helpless, not the past
Victorious with banners, called her on ;
And she assembled not her sons alone

From city and hamlet, coast and heath and hill,
But deep within her bosom, deeper still
Than any fear could search, than any hope could
     blind,
Beyond all clamours of her recent day,
Hot smouldering of the faction and the fray,
She summoned her own soul. In the hour of
     night,
In the hush that felt the armed tread of her foes,
Like a star, silent out of seas, it rose.

Most human France ! In those clear eyes of
     light
Was vision of the issue, and all the cost
To the last drop of generous blood, the last
Tears of the orphan and the widow ; and yet
She shrank not from the terror of the debt,
Seeing what else were with the cause undone,
The very skies barred with an iron threat,
The very mind of freedom lost
Beneath that shadow bulked across the sun.
Therefore did she abstain
From all that had renowned her, all that won
The world's delight : thought-stilled
With deep reality to the heart she burned,
And took upon her all the load of pain

Foreknown ; and her sons turned
From wife's and children's kiss
Simply, and steady-willed
With quiet eyes, with courage keen and clear,
Faced Eastward.—If an English voice she hear,
That has no speech worthy of her, let this
Be of that day remembered, with what pride
Our ancient island thrilled to the oceans wide,
And our hearts leapt to know that England then,
Equal in faith of free and loyal men,
Stept to her side.

EDITH CAVELL

SHE was binding the wounds of her enemies
    when they came—
The lint in her hand unrolled.
They battered the door with their rifle-butts,
    crashed it in :
She faced them gentle and bold.

They haled her before the judges where they sat
    In their places, helmet on head.
With question and menace the judges assailed
    her, " Yes,
I have broken your law," she said.

" I have tended the hurt and hidden the hunted,
    have done
    As a sister does to a brother,
Because of a law that is greater than that you
    have made,
    Because I could do none other.

" Deal as you will with me. This is my choice to
 the end,
 To live in the life I vowed."
" She is self-confessed," they cried, " she is self-
 condemned.
 She shall die that the rest may be cowed."

In the terrible hour of the dawn, when the veins
 are cold,
 They led her forth to the wall.
" I have loved my land," she said, " but it is
 not enough :
 Love requires of me all.

" I will empty my heart of the bitterness, hating
 none."
 And sweetness filled her brave
With a vision of understanding beyond the hour
 That knelled to the waiting grave.

They bound her eyes, but she stood as if she
 shone.
 The rifles it was that shook
When the hoarse command rang out. They
 could not endure
 That last, that defenceless look.

And the officer strode and pistolled her surely,
    ashamed,
  That men, seasoned in blood,
Should quail at a woman, only a woman,—
    dead
  As a flower stamped in the mud.

And now that the deed was securely done, in
    the night
  When none had known her fate,
They answered those that had striven for her,
    day by day :
  " It is over, you come too late."

And with many words and sorrowful-phrased
    excuse
  Argued their German right
To kill, most legally ; hard though the duty be,
  The law must assert its might.

Only a woman ! yet she had pity on them,
  The victim offered slain
To the gods of fear that they worship. Leave
    them there,
  Red hands, to clutch their gain !

She bewailed not herself, and we will bewail her
    not
  But with tears of pride rejoice
That an English soul was found so crystal-clear
  To be triumphant voice

Of the human heart that dares adventure all
  But live to itself untrue,
And beyond all laws sees love as the light in the
    night,
  As the star it must answer to.

The hurts she healed, the thousands comforted
    —these
  Make a fragrance of her fame.
But because she stept to her star right on
    through death
  It is Victory speaks her name.

MID-ATLANTIC

IF this were all !—A dream of dread
Ran through me ; I watched the waves that fled
Pale-crested out of hollows black,
The hungry lift of helpless waves,
A million million tossing graves,
A wilderness without a track
Beneath the barren moon :
If this were all !
The stars of night remotely strewn
Looked on that restless heave and fall.
I seemed with them to watch this old
Bright planet through the ages rolled,
Self-tortured, burning splendours vain
And fevered with its greeds insane
And with the blood of peoples red ;
I watched it, grown an ember cold,
Join in the dancing of the dead.

The chilly half-moon sank ; the sound
Of naked surges roared around,

G

And through my heart the darkness poured
Surges as of a sea unshored.
O somewhere far and lost from light
Blind Europe battled in the night !
Then sudden through the darkness came
The vision of a child,
A child with feet as light as flame
Who ran across the bitter waves,
Across the tumbling of the graves—
With arms stretched out he smiled.
I drank the wine of life again,
I breathed among my brother men,
I felt the human fire.
I knew that I must serve the will
Of beauty and love and wisdom still ;
Though all my hopes were overthrown,
Though universes turned to stone,
I have my being in this alone
And die in that desire.

On board the "Lusitania,"
    December, 1914.

THE CAUSE

Out of these throes that search and sear
What is it so deep arises in us
Above the shaken thoughts of fear,—
Whatever thread the Fates may spin us,—
Above the horror that would drown
And tempest that would strike us down ?

It is to stand in cleansing light,
The cloud of dullard habit lifted,
To use a certainty of sight
And breathe an air by peril sifted,
The things that once we deemed of price
Consumed in smoke of sacrifice.

It is to feel the world we knew
Changed to a wonder past our knowing ;
The grass, the trees, the skiey blue,
The very stones are inly glowing
With something infinite behind
These shadows, ardently divined.

We went our ways ; each bosom bore
Its spark of separate desire ;
But each now kindles to the core
With faith from this transfusing fire,
Whereto our inmost longings run
To be made infinitely one

With that which nothing can destroy,
Which lives when all is crushed and taken,
The home of dearer than our joy,
By all save by the soul forsaken
Who strips her clean of doubt and care
Because she breathes her native air,

Yet not in scorn of lovely earth
And human sweetness born of living,
For these are grown of dearer worth,
A gift more precious in the giving,
Since through this raiment's hues and lines
The glory of the spirit shines.

Faces of radiant youth, that go
Like rivers singing to the sea !
You count no careful cost ; you know ;
Of that far secret you are free ;
And life in you its splendour spending
Sings the stars' song that has no ending.

BEFORE THE DAWN

BEFORE THE DAWN

Blacker the night grows ere the dawn be risen,
Keener the cost, and fiercer yet the fight.
But hark! above the thunder and the terror
A trumpet blowing splendid through the night.

It is the challenge of our dead undying
Calling, *Remember! we have died for you.*
It is the cry of perilled earth's hereafter—
Sons of our sons—*Be glorious, be true!*

Now in the hour when either world is witness,
Never or now shall we be proven great,
Rise to the height of all our strain and story,
Ay, and beyond; for we ourselves are Fate.

GALLIPOLI

Isles of the Aegean, Troy, and waters of Helles-
    pont !
  You we have known from of old,
Since boyhood stammering glorious Greek was
    entranced
  In the tale that Homer told.
There scornful Achilles towered and flamed
    through the battle,
  Defying the gods ; and there
Hector armed, and Andromache proudly held
    up his boy to him,
  Knowing not yet despair.

We beheld them as presences moving beautiful
    and swift
  In the radiant morning of Time,
Far from reality, far from dulness of daily doing
  And from cities of fog and grime ;—
Unattainable day-dream, heroes, gods and
    goddesses
  Matched in splendour of war,

Days of a vanished world, days of a grandeur
  perished,
  Days that should bloom no more.

But now shall our boyhood learn to tell a new
  tale,
  And a new song shall be sung,
And the sound of it shall praise not magnifi-
  cence of old time
  But the glory and the greatness of the young.
Deeds of this our own day, marvellous deeds of
  our own blood ;
  Sons that their sires excel,
Lightly going into peril and taking death by
  the hand ;—
  Of these they shall sing, they shall tell.

How in ships sailing the famed Mediterranean
  From armed banks of Nile
Men from far homes in sunny Austral Dominions
  And the misty mother-isle,
Met in the great cause, joined in the vast adven-
  ture,
  Saw first in April skies
Beyond storied islands, Gallipoli's promontory
  Impregnably ridged, arise.

And how from the belly of the black ship,
   driven beneath
   Towering scarp and scaur
Hailing hidden rages of fire in terrible gusts
   On the murdered space of shore,
Into the water they leapt, they rushed and
   across the beach,
   With impetuous shout, all
Inspired beyond men, climbed and were over
   the crest
   As a flame leaps over a wall.

Not all the gods in heaven's miraculous panoply
   Could have hindered or stayed them, so
Irresistibly came they, scaled the unscaleable
   and sprang
   To stab the astonished foe,
Marvellous doers of deeds, lifted past our ima-
   gining
   To a world where death is nought!
As spirit against spirit, as a liberated element,
   As fire in flesh they fought.

Now to the old twilight and pale legendary
   glories,
   By our own youth outdone,

Those shores recede ; not there, but in memory
  everlasting
The immortal heights were won.
Of them that triumphed, of them that fell,
  there is only now
Silence, and sleep, and fame,
And in night's immensity far on that promon-
  tory's altar
An invisibly burning flame.

THE DISTANT GUNS

NEGLIGENTLY the cart-track descends into the
   valley ;
The drench of the rain has passed and the clover
   breathes ;
Scents are abroad ; in the valley a mist whitens
Along the hidden river, where the evening
   smiles.
The trees are asleep, their shadows are longer
   and longer,
Melting blue in the tender twilight ; above,
In a pallor, barred with lilac and ashen cloud,
Delicate as a spirit the young moon brightens ;
And distant a bell intones the hour of peace,
Where roofs of the village, gray and red, cluster
In leafy dimness. Peace, old as the world !
The crickets shrilling in the high wet grass,
And gnats, clouding upon the frail wild roses,
Murmur of you ; but hark ! like a shudder upon
   the air,
Ominous and alien, knocking on the farther
   hills

As with airy hammers, the ghosts of terrible
    sound,—
Guns! From afar they are knocking on human
    hearts
Everywhere over the silent evening country,
Knocking with fear and dark presentiment.
  Only
The moon's beauty, where no life nor joy is,
Brightening softly and knowing nothing, has
    peace.

ARC-EN-BARROIS, 1916.

MEN OF VERDUN

THERE are five men in the moonlight
  That by their shadows stand :
Three hobble humped on crutches,
  And two lack each a hand.

Frogs somewhere near the roadside
  Chorus a chant absorbed ;
But a hush breathes out of the dream-light
  That far in heaven is orbed.

It is gentle as sleep falling
  And wide as thought can span,
The ancient peace and wonder
  That brims the heart of man.

Beyond the hills it shines now
  On no peace but the dead,
On reek of trenches thunder-shocked,
Tense fury of wills in wrestle locked,
  A chaos crumbled red !

The five men in the moonlight
　Chat, joke, or gaze apart.
They talk of days and comrades;
　But each one hides his heart.

They wear clean cap and tunic,
　As when they went to war;
A gleam comes where the medal's pinned:
　But they will fight no more.

The shadows, maimed and antic,
　Gesture and shape distort,
Like mockery of a demon dumb
Out of the hell-din whence they come
　That dogs them for his sport.

But as if dead men were risen
　And stood before me there
With a terrible flame about them blown
　In beams of spectral air,

I see them, men transfigured
　As in a dream, dilate
Fabulous with the Titan-throb
　Of battling Europe's fate;

For history's hushed before them,
  And legend flames afresh.
Verdun, the name of thunder,
  Is written on their flesh.

LA PATRIE

THROUGH storm-blown gloom the subtle light
   persists ;
Shapes of tumultuous, ghostly cloud appear,
Trailing a dark shower from hill-drenching
   mists :
Dawn, desolate in its majesty, is here.

But ere the wayside trees show leaf and form
Invisible larks in all the air around
Ripple their songs up through the gloom and
   storm,
As if the baulked light had won wings of sound !

A wounded soldier on his stretcher waits
His turn for the ambulance, by the glimmering
   rails.
He is wrapped in a rough brown blanket, like
   his mates.
Over him the dawn broadens, the cloud pales.

H

Muscular, swart, bearded, and quite still,
He lies, too tired to think, to wonder. Drops
From a leaf fall by him. For spent nerve and
    will
The world of shattering and stunned effort stops.

He feels the air, song-thrilled and fresh and
    dim,
And close about him smells the rainy soil.
It is ever-living Earth recovers him,
Friend and companion of old, fruitful toil.

He is patient with her patience. Hurt, he takes
Strength from her rooted, still tenacities.
The will to heal, that secretly remakes,
Like slumber, holds his dark, contented eyes.

For she, though—never reckoning of the cost—
Full germs of all profusion she prepares,
Knows tragic hours, too, parching famine, frost
And wreck; and in her children's hurt she
    shares.

Build what we may, house us in lofty mind's
Palaces, wean the fine-wrought spirit apart,
Earth touches where the fibre throbs, and winds
The threads about us of her infinite heart.

And some dear ground with its own changing
  sky,
As if it were our feeling flesh, is wrought
Into the very body's dignity
And private colour of least conscious thought.

O when that loud invader burned and bruised
This ordered land's old kindness, with brute
  blows
Shamed and befouled and plundered and abused,
Was it not Earth that in her soldier rose

And armed him, terrible and simple? He
Takes his wound, mute as Earth is, yet as
  strong.—
The funeral clouds trail, wet wind shakes the
  tree,
But all the wild air of the dawn is song.

LATRECY, 1916.

THE DEPORTATION

I

In vain, in vain, in vain !
Conqueror, you are conquered : though you
    grind
Those bodies, heel on neck ; and though you
    twist
Out of them the exquisite last wrench of pain,
They rise, they rise again,
Rise quivering and eternally resist
All cunning that all cruelty can find
To mock the heart and lacerate the mind
In vain, in vain !

II

The train stands packed for exile, truck on
    truck.
Men thronged like oxen, pressed against each
    other,
With worse than anger in their dangerous eyes,

Look on their drivers, armed and helmeted,—
Then forget all in sudden stormy cries
As past the bayonets sister, wife, and mother
Strain up to them, clutch fingers tight, are
  struck
And beaten back, but struggle and press again,
Catch desolated kisses, fight for breath
To sob their widowed hearts out in a word
Their man shall hear, reckless of wound or
  death
So they come nigh him ; a farewell insane,
A passion as if the earth that bore them heard
And in her bones groaned ! And white children
  held
On shoulders where the torn dress hangs in
  strips
Cry Father ! and mute answers wring the lips
Of the exiles, in their torture still unquelled.

A whistle screams. The guards drive, shout,
  beat. Then
An inspiration like an ecstasy
Seizes these women, and they rush to throw
Their sobbing bodies prone upon the tracks
Before the panting engine. If their men
Into that night of slavery must go,

They'll be with death before them! Prostrate
    there,
Tear-blinded, with tense arms and heaving
    backs,
Young wife and child and mother of grey hair
Clutch the rails, anguished and athirst to die,
While over them the towering engine throbs,
Blind, ignorant, deaf, and ready. But you
    spare
Such easiness of end, you who did this
Which the sun looked on, and which History
Shall see for ever. Though they cling with sobs
To their own earth, frenzied and bleeding, swift
They are harried up; the bayonets prise and
    lift
And tear away their hands' despairing grasp;
They are tossed on either side: at the engine's
    hiss
The wheels begin that road which curses pave
Between those piteous heaps that cry and gasp
Helpless, and cheated even of their grave.

III

But something lives and burns
More perilous to assail
Than flesh of bodies frail :
It waits and it returns.
And when in the night you dream
Of the day that you did this thing,
When you see those eyes and the bayonet's
    gleam
And the shrieks to your very heart's blood ring
As you do your deed in your dream again,
The soul of the race that you racked, to do
Your Lord's command, that you thought to
    have cowed,
Shall sharpen the bitterness thrice for you
As it rises before you, crying aloud :
You did it in vain, in vain !

THE BELLS OF YPRES

On the road to Ypres, on the long road,
Marching strong,
We'll sing a song of Ypres, of her glory
And her wrong.
Proud rose her towers in the old time,
Long ago.
Trees stood on her ramparts, and the water
Lay below.
Shattered are the towers into potsherds—
Jumbled stones.
Underneath the ashes that were rafters
Whiten bones.
Blood is in the cellar where the wine was,
On the floor.
Rats run on the pavement where the wives met
At the door.
But in Ypres there's an army that is biding,
Seen of none,
You'd never hear their tramp, nor see their
    shadow
In the sun.

Thousands of the dead men there are waiting
Through the night,
Waiting for a bugle in the cold dawn
Blown for fight.
Listen when the bugle's calling Forward !
They'll be found,
Dead men, risen in battalions
From underground,
Charging with us home, and through the foemen
Driving fear
Swifter than the madness in a madman,
As they hear
Dead men ring the bells of Ypres
For a sign,
Hear the bells and fear them in the Hun-land
Over Rhine !

ENGLAND'S POET

Written for the Shakespeare Tercentenary

To other voices, other majesties,
Removed this while, Peace shall resort again.
But he was with us in our darkest pain
And stormiest hour : his faith royally dyes
The colours of our cause ; his voice replies
To all our doubt, dear spirit ! heart and vein
Of England's old adventure ! his proud strain
Rose from our earth to the sea-breathing skies.

Even over chaos and the murdering roar
Comes that world-winning music, whose full
   stops
Sounded all man, the bestial and divine ;
Terrible as thunder, fresh as April drops.
He stands, he speaks, the soul-transfigured sign
Of all our story, on the English shore.

GOING WEST

Just as I came
Into the empty, westward-facing room,
A sudden gust blew wide
The tall window ; at once
A shock of sudden light, vibrating like a flame,
Entered, as if it were the wind's bright spirit
Stealing to me upon some secret quest.
The wonder of the West
Burst open ; under dark and rushing cloud
That rained illumined drops, it glorified
Each corner where so dazzlingly it struck :
The shadows cowered, the brilliance overflowed.
As suddenly, all faded.
Wet, wild air blew in
At the idly-swinging door
Stormily crumpled fallen shreds of leaves,
Dried scarlet and burnt yellow and ashy brown :
They fluttered in like fears and blew across the
    floor.
And I, to the heart invaded,
Felt as that wild light palpitated through me

And died in a moment down,
Exalted by a visionary fear
That from the light more than the shadow fell ;
A divination of splendid spirits near,
Of glorious parting and of great farewell.

THE BEREAVED

WE grudged not those that were dearer than
    all we possessed,
  Lovers, brothers, sons.
Our hearts were full, and out of a full heart
  We gave our belovèd ones.

Because we loved, we gave. In the hardest
    hour
  When at last—so much unsaid
In the eyes—they went, simply, with tender
    smile,
  Our hearts to the end they read.

They to their deeds ! To things that their soul
    hated,
  And yet to splendours won
From smoking hell by the spirit that moved in
    them ;
  But we to endure alone.

Their hearts rested on ours ; their homing
    thoughts
  Met ours in the still of the night.
We ached with the ache of the long waiting, and
    throbbed
  With the throbs of the surging fight.

O had we failed them, then were we desolate
    now
  And separated indeed.
What should have comforted, what should have
    helped us then
  In the time of our bitter need !

But now, though sorrow be ever fresh, sorrow
  Is tender as love ; it knows
That of love it was born, and Love with the
    shining eyes
  The hard way chose.

And out of deeps eternal, night and day,
  A strength our sorrow frees,
Flooding us, full as the tide up the rivers flows
  From the depth of the silent seas ;

A strength that is mightier far than we, yet a
    strength
  Whereof our spirit is breath,
Hope of the world, that is strange to hazard
  . and fear,
  To the wounds of Time, and Death.

THE SIBYLS

RENDING the waters of a night unknown
The ship with tireless pulses bore me,
On the shadowy deck musing late and lone,
Over waste ocean.
The rustling of the cordage in the dewy wind
And the sound of idle surges
Falling prolonged and for ever again up-thrown
Drowsed me ; I slept, I dreamed.

Out of the seas that streamed
In ghostly turbulence moving and glimmering
    about me
I saw the rising of vast and visionary forms.

Like clouds, like continents of cloud, they rose
August as the shape of storms
In the silence before the thunder, or of moun-
    tains
Alone in a sky of sunken light : they rose
Slowly, with shrouded grandeur

Of queenly bosom and shoulder ; and afar
Their countenances were lifted, although veiled,
Although heavy as with thought and with
  silence,
In the heights where dimly gathered
Star upon solitary star.

And it seemed to me, as I dreamed,
That these were the forms of the Sibyls of old,
Prophetesses whose eyes were aflame with in-
  terior fire,
Who passionately prophesied and none com-
  prehended,
In the womb of whose thought was quickened
  the world's desire,
Who saw, and because they saw, chastised
With voices terribly chanting on the wind
The folly of the faithlessness of men.

But not as they haunted then
In cavernous and wild places,
Each inaccessibly sequestered
And sought with furtive steps
Through wizard leaves of whispering laurel
  feared,

I

Now to me they appeared.
But rather like Queens of fabulous dominion
Like Queens, voices of a voiceless people,
Queens of old time, with aweing faces,
With burdened brows but with proud eyes,
Assembled in solemn parley, to shape
Futurity and the nations' glory and doom,
They were met in the night together.

And lo ! beneath them
The immeasureable circle of the gloom
Phantasmally disclosed
In apparition all the coasts of the world,
Veined with rivers afar to the frozen mountains.
And I saw the shadow of maniac Death
Like a reveller there stagger glutted and
    gloating.
I saw murdered cities
That raised like a stiffened arm
One blackened tower to heaven ; I saw
Processions of the homeless crawling into the
    distances ;
And sullen leagues of interminable battle ;
And peoples arming afar ; the very earth,
The very bowels of the earth infected
With the rages and the agonies of men.

For a moment the vision gleamed, and then
  was gone:
Gloom rushed down like rain.
But out of the midst of the darkness
My flesh was aware of a sound,
The peopled-sound of moving millions
And the voices of human pain.

I lifted my gaze to the Sibyls,
The Sibyls of the Continents, where they rose
Looking one on another.
Ancestral Asia, mother of musing mind,
Was there ; and over against her
Towered in the gates of the West a shape
Of youth gigantic, troubled and vigilant ;
Patient with eager dumbness in dark eyes,
Africa rose ; and ardent out of the South
The youngest of those great sisters ; and proud,
With fame upon her for mantle, and regal-
  browed,
The stature of Europe old.

It seemed they listened to the murmur
Of the anguished lands beneath them
In sombre reverberation rising and upward
  rolled.

Everywhere battle and arming for battle,
Famine and torture, odour of burning and
  blood,
Doubt, hatred, terror,
Rage and lamenting !
I heard sweet Pity crying between the earth
  and sky :
But who had leisure for her call ? or who
  hearkened to her cry ?

Not with our vision, and not with our horizon
The gaze of the Sibyls was filled.
Their trouble was trouble beyond the shaping
  of our fear,
Their hope full-sailed upon oceans beyond
  our ken ;
Their thoughts were the thoughts that build
Towers for the dawn unseen.

But nearer than ever before
They drew to each other, sister to shrouded
  sister,
Queen to superb Queen.
What counsel took they together ? or what
  word

Of power and of parturition
Passed their lips ? What saw they,
Conferring among the stars ?
My blood tingled, and I heard
Syllables, O too vast
For capacity of my ears, yet within me,
In the innermost bones and caves of my being
I felt a voice like the voice of a sea,
And the sound of it seemed to be crying :
' Endure !
Humble yourselves, O dreamers of dreams,
In whose bosom is peril fiercer than fire or beast,
Humble yourselves, O desolaters of your own
    dreams,
Then arise and remember !
Though now you cry in astonishment and
    anguish
 What have we done to the beauty of the world
That it ruins about us in ashes and blood ? '
Remember the Spirit that moulded and made
    you
In the beauty of the body
Shaped as the splendour of speech to thought,
The Spirit that wills with one desire,
With infinite else unsatisfied desire,
Peace, not made by conquerors and armies,

Peace born in the soul, that asks not shelter or
    a pillow,
The peace of truth, unshaken amid the thunder,
Unaffrighted by fury of shrivelling fire,
And neither time nor tempest
Neither slumber nor calamity,
Neither rending of the flesh nor breaking of the
    heart,
Shall stay you from that desire."

That sound floated like a cloud in heaven,
Lingering ; and like an answer
Came the sound of the rushing of spirits trium-
    phant,
Of young men dying for a cause.

I lifted my eyes in wonder.
And silence filled me.
And with the silence I was aware
Of a breath moving in the glimmer of the air.
The stars had vanished ; but again
I beheld those Sibyls august
Over stilled ocean,
And on their faces the dawn.
Even as I looked, they lifted up their heads,

They lifted their heads, like eagles
That slowly shake and widen their wondrous
   wings;
They arose and vanished like the stars.
The light of the changed world, the world new-
   born,
Brimmed over the silence of the seas;
But even in the rising of its beam
I remembered the light in their eyes.

TO THE END

BECAUSE the time has stript us bare
Of all things but the thing we are,
Because our faith requires us whole
And we are seen to the very soul,
Rejoice! from now all meaner fears are fled.

Because we have no prize to win
Auguster than the truth within,
And by consuming of the dross
Magnificently lose our loss,
Rejoice! we have not vainly borne and bled.

Because we chose beyond recall
And for dear honour hazard all,
And summoned to the last attack
Refuse to falter or look back,
Rejoice! we die, the Cause is never dead.

THE NEW WORLD

MORN LIKE A THOUSAND SHINING SPEARS

MORN like a thousand shining spears
Terrible in the East appears.
O hide me, leaves of lovely gloom,
Where the young Dreams like lilies bloom !

What is this music that I lose
Now, in a world of fading clues ?
What wonders from beyond the seas
And wild Arabian fragrancies ?

In vain I turn me back to where
Stars made a palace of the air.
In vain I hide my face away
From the too bright invading Day.

That which is come requires of me
My utter truth and mystery.
Return, you dreams, return to Night :
My lover is the arméd Light.

123

THE NEW WORLD

To the people of the United States

Now is the time of the splendour of Youth and
    Death.
The spirit of man grows grander than men knew.
The unbearable burden is borne, the impossible
    done ;
Though harder is yet to do
Before this agony end, and that be won
We seek through blinding battle, in choking
    breath,—
The New World, seen in vision ! Land of lands,
In the midst of storms that desolate and divide,
In the hour of the breaking heart, O far-
    descried,
You build our courage, you hold up our hands.

Men of America, you that march to-day
Through roaring London, supple and lean of
    limb,
Glimpsed in the crowd I saw you, and in your eye
Something alert and grim,

As knowing on what stern call you march away
To the wrestle of nations ; saw your heads held
  high
And, that same moment, far in a glittering
  beam
High over old and storied Westminster
The Stars and Stripes with England's flag astir,
Sisterly twined and proud on the air astream.

Men of America, what do you see ? Is it old
Towers of fame and grandeur time-resigned ?
The frost of custom's backward-gazing thought ?
Seek closer ! You shall find
Miracles hour by hour in silence wrought ;
Births, and awakenings ; dyings never tolled ;
Invisible crumble and fall of prison-bars. ·
O, wheresoever his home, new or decayed,
Man is older than all the things he has made
And yet the youngest spirit beneath the stars.

Rock-cradled, white, and soaring out of the
  sea,
I behold again the fabulous city arise,
Manhattan ! Queen of thronged and restless
  bays
And of daring ships is she.

O lands beyond, that into the sunset gaze,
Limitless, teeming continent of surmise !
I drink again that diamond air, I thrill
To the lure of a wonder more than the wondrous
    past,
And see before me ages yet more vast
Rising, to challenge heart and mind and will.

What sailed they out to seek, who of old came
To that bare earth and wild, unhistoried coast ?
Not gold, nor granaries, nay, nor a halcyon ease
For the weary and tempest-tost :
The unshaken soul they sought, possessed in
    peace.
What seek we now, and hazard all on the aim ?
In the heart of man is the undiscovered earth
Whose hope's our compass ; sweet with glorious
    passion
Of men's good-will ; a world to forge and
    fashion
Worthy the things we have seen and brought
    to birth.

Taps of the Drum ! Now once again they beat :
And the answer comes ; a continent arms.
    Dread,

Pity, and Grief, there is no escape. The call
Is the call of the risen Dead.
Terrible year of the nations' trampling feet !
An angel has blown his trumpet over all
From the ends of the earth, from East to utter-
  most West,
Because of the soul of man, that shall not fail,
That will not make refusal, or turn, or quail,
No, nor for all calamity, stay its quest.

And here, here too, is the New World, born of
  pain
In destiny-spelling hours. The old world breaks
Its mould, and life runs fierce and fluid, a stream
That floods, dissolves, re-makes.
Each pregnant moment, charged to its extreme,
Quickens unending future, and all's vain
But the onward mind, that dares the oncoming
  years
And takes their storm, a master. Life shall then
Transfigure Time with yet more marvellous men.
Hail to the sunrise ! Hail to the Pioneers !

THE SOWER

(Eastern France)

FAMILIAR, year by year, to the creaking wain
Is the long road's level ridge above the plain.
To-day a battery comes with horses and guns
On the straight road, that under the poplars
    runs,
At leisurely pace, the guns with mouths declined,
Harness merrily ringing, and dust behind.
Makers of widows, makers of orphans, they
Pass to their burial business, alert and gay.

But down in the field, where sun has the furrow
    dried,
Is a man who walks in the furrow with even
    stride.
At every step, with elbow jerked across,
He scatters seed in a quick, deliberate toss,
The immemorial gesture of Man confiding
To Earth, that restores tenfold in a season's
    gliding.
He is grave and patient, sowing his children's
    bread :
He treads the kindly furrow, nor turns his head.

STONEHENGE

GAUNT on the cloudy plain
Stand the great Stones,
Dwarfed in the vast reach
Of a sky that owns

All the measure of earth
Within its cloud-hung cave.
Dumb stands the Circle
As on a God's grave.

But clattering with horses
Up from the valley,
With horses and horsemen
At a trot, gaily

Dragging the limbered guns,
Youth comes riding,—
Easy sits, mettlesome
Horses bestriding.

K

STONEHENGE

Fast come the twinkling hoofs,
Light wheels and guns,
Invading the upland,
And sweep past the Stones.

Giant those shapes now
Over them tower,—
Time's dark stature
Over Youth's fleet hour.

Ribs of dismemoried Earth,
Guard what you may !
The Immortals also
Pass, nor stay.

GUNS AT THE FRONT

MAN, simple and brave, easily confiding,
Giving his all, glad of the sun's sweetness,
Heeding little of pitiful incompleteness,
Mending life with laughter and cheerful chiding,

Where is he ?—I see him not, but I hear
Sounds, charged with nothing but death and
    maiming ;
Earth and sky empty of all but flaming
Bursts, and shocks that stun the waiting ear ;

Monsters roaring aloud with hideous vastness,
Nothing, Nothing, Nothing ! And man that
    made them
Mightier far than himself, has stooped, and
    obeyed them,
Schooled his mind to endure its own aghastness,

Serving death, destruction, and things inert,—
He the soarer, free of heavens to roam in,

He whose heart has a world of light to home in,
Confounding day with darkness, flesh with dirt.

O, dear indeed the cause that so can prove him,
Pitilessly self-tested ! If no cause beaconed
Beyond this chaos, better he bled unreckoned,
With his own monsters bellowing madness above
  him.

THE WITNESSES

I

LADS in the loose blue,
Crutched, with limping feet,
With bandaged arm, that roam
To-day the bustling street,

You humble us with your gaze,
Calm, confiding, clear ;
You humble us with a smile
That says nothing but cheer.

Our souls are scarred with you !
Yet, though we suffered all
You have suffered, all were vain
To atone, or to recall

The robbèd future, or build
The maimed body again
Whole, or ever efface
What men have done to men.

II

Each body of straight youth,
Strong, shapely, and marred,
Shines as out of a cloud
Of storm and splintered shard,

Of chaos, torture, blood,
Fire, thunder, and stench :
And the savage shattering noise
Of churned and shaken trench

Echoes through myriad hearts
In the dumb lands behind ;—
Silent wailing, and bitter
Tears of the world's mind !

You stand upon each threshold
Without complaint.—What pen
Dares to write half the deeds
That men have done to men ?

III

Must we be humbled more ?
Peace, whose olive seems
A tree of hope and heaven,
Of answered prayers and dreams,

Peace has her own hid wounds ;
She also grinds and maims.
And must we bear and share
Those old continued shames ?

Not only the body's waste
But the mind's captivities—
Crippled, sore, and starved—
The ignorant victories

Of the visionless, who serve
No cause, and fight no foe !
Is a cruelty less sure
Because its ways are slow ?

Now we have eyes to see.
Shall we not use them then ?
These bright wounds witness us
What men may do to men.

I AM HERE, AND YOU

I AM here, and you ;
The sun blesses us through
Leaves made of light.
The air is in your hair ;
You hold a flower.

O worlds, that roll through night,
O Time, O terrible year,
Where surges of fury and fear
Rave, to us you gave
This island-hour.

DARK WIND

In the middle of the night, waking, I was aware
Of the Wind like one riding through black wastes
   of the air,
Moodily riding, ever faster, he recked not where.

The windows rattled aloud : a door clashed and
   sprang ;
And the ear in fear waited to feel the inert clang
Strike the shaken darkness, a cruelty and a
  pang.

I was hurt with pity of things that have no will
   of their own,
Lifted in lives of others and cast on bruising
   stone :
I feared the Wind, coming a power from worlds
   unknown.

It was like a great ship now, abandoned, her
    crew dead,
Driving in gulfs of sky ; it staggered above and
    sped ;
I lay in the deeps and heard it rushing over
    my head.

And the helpless shaking of window and door's
    desolate rebound
Seemed like tossing and lifting of bodies lost
    and drowned
In the huge indifferent swell, in the waters'
    wandering sound.

HUNGER

I COME among the peoples like a shadow.
I sit down by each man's side.

None sees me, but they look on one another,
And know that I am there.

My silence is like the silence of the tide
That buries the playground of children ;

Like the deepening of frost in the slow night,
When birds are dead in the morning.

Armies trample, invade, destroy,
With guns roaring from earth and air.

I am more terrible than armies,
I am more feared than the cannon.

Kings and chancellors give commands ;
I give no command to any ;

But I am listened to more than kings
And more than passionate orators.

I unswear words, and undo deeds.
Naked things know me.

I am first and last to be felt of the living.
I am Hunger.

STRIKE STONE ON STEEL

STRIKE stone on steel,
Fire replies.
Strike men that feel,
The answer is in their eyes.

Powers that are willed to break
The spirit in limbs of pain,
See what spirit you wake !
Strike, and strike again !

You hammer sparks to a flame,
And the flame scorches your hand.
You have given the feeble an aim,
You have made the sick to stand.

You shape by stroke on stroke
Man mightier than he knew ;
And the fire your hammer woke
Is a life that is death to you.

SPRING HAS LEAPT INTO SUMMER

SPRING has leapt into Summer.
A glory has gone from the green.
The flush of the poplar has sobered out,
The flame in the leaf of the lime is dulled :
But I am thinking of the young men
Whose faces are no more seen.

Where is the pure blossom
That fell and refused to grow old ?
The clustered radiance, perfumed whiteness,
Silent singing of joy in the blue ?
—I am thinking of the young men
Whose splendour is under the mould.

Youth, the wonder of the world,
Open-eyed at an opened door,
When the world is as honey in the flower, and
  as wine
To the heart, and as music newly begun !

O the young men, the myriads of the young men,
Whose beauty returns no more !

Spring will come, when the Earth remembers,
In sun-bursts after the rain,
And the leaf be fresh and lovely on the bough,
And the myriad shining blossom be born :
But I shall be thinking of the young men
Whose eyes will not shine on us again.

THE ENGLISH YOUTH

THERE is a dimness fallen on old fames.
Our hearts are solemnized with dearer names
Than Time is bright with : we have not heard
   alone,
Or read of it in books ; it is our own
Eyes that have seen this wonder ; like a song,
It is in our mouths for ever. There was wrong
Done, and the world shamed. Honour blew the
   call ;
And each one's answer was as natural
And quiet as the needle's to the pole.
Who gave must give himself entire and whole.
So, books were shut ; and young dreams shaken
   out
In cold air ; dear ambitions done without,
And a stark duty shouldered. And yet they
Who now must narrow to their arduous day
Did not forget their nurture, nor the kind
Muses of earth, nor joys of eager mind,—
Graced in their comradeship, and prizing more
Life's beauty, and all the sweetness at the core,

Because of that loathed business they were set
To do and finish. It was the world's debt,
Claiming all: but they knew, and would not wince
From that exaction on their flesh ; and since
They did not seek for glory, our hearts add
A more than glory to that hope they had
And gloriously and terribly achieved.

O histories of old time, half-believed,
None needs to wrong the modesty of truth
In matching with your legend England's youth.
But all renown that fearless arms could win
For proud adventuring wondrous Paladin
Is glimmering laurel now : Romance, that was
The coloured air of a forgotten cause
About the heads of heroes dead and bright,
Shines home. We are accompanied with light
Because of youth among us ; and the name
Of man is touched with an ethereal flame ;
There is a newness in the world begun,
A difference in the setting of the sun.
Oh, though we stumble in blinding tears, and
   though
The beating of our hearts may never know
Absence in pangs more desolately keen,
Yet blessed are our eyes because they have seen.

L

OXFORD IN WAR-TIME

WHAT alters you, familiar lawn and tower,
Arched alley, and garden green to the grey wall
With crumbling crevice and the old wine-red
   flower,
Solitary in summer sun ? for all

Is like a dream : I tread on dreams ! No stir
Of footsteps, voices, laughter ! Even the chime
Of many-memoried bells is lonelier
In this neglected ghostliness of Time.

What stealing touch of separation numb
Absents you ? Yet my heart springs up to adore
The shrining of your soul, that is become
Nearer and oh, far dearer than before.

It is as if I looked on the still face
Of a Mother, musing where she sits alone.
She is with her sons, she is not in this place ;
She is gone out into far lands unknown.

Because that filled horizon occupies
Her heart with mute prayer and divining fear,
Therefore her hands so calm lie, and her eyes
See nothing ; and men wonder at her here :

But far in France ; on the torn Flanders plain ;
By Sinai ; in the Macedonian snows ;
The fly-plagued sands of Tigris, heat and rain ;
On wandering water, where the black squall
   blows

Less danger than the bright wave ambushes,
She bears it out. All the long day she bears
And the sudden hour of instant challenges
To act, that searches all men, no man spares.

She is with her sons, leaving a virtue gone
Out of her sacred places : what she bred
Lives other life than this, that sits alone,
Though still in dream starrily visited !

For O in youth she lives, not in her age.
Her soul is with the springtime and the young ;
And she absents her from the learned page,
Studious of high histories yet unsung,

More passionately prized than wisdom's book
Because her own. Her faith is in those eyes
That clear into the gape of hell can look,
Putting to proof ancient philosophies

Such as the virgin Muses would rehearse
Beside the silvery, swallow-haunted stream,
Under the grey towers. But immortal verse
Is now exchanged for its immortal theme—

Victory ; proud loss ; and the enduring mind ;
Youth, that has passed all praises, and has won
More than renown, being that which faith
    divined,
Reality more radiant than the sun.

She gave, she gives, more than all anchored days
Of dedicated lore, of storied art ;
And she resigns her beauty to men's gaze
To mask the riches of her bleeding heart.

THE DEAD TO THE LIVING

O you that still have rain and sun,
Kisses of children and of wife
And the good earth to tread upon,
And the mere sweetness that is life,
Forget not us, who gave all these
For something dearer, and for you.
Think in what cause we crossed the seas !
Remember, he who fails the Challenge
Fails us too.

Now in the hour that shows the strong—
The soul no evil powers affray—
Drive straight against embattled Wrong :
Faith knows but one, the hardest, way.
Endure ; the end is worth the throe.
Give, give, and dare ; and again dare !
On, to that Wrong's great overthrow.
We are with you, of you ; we the pain
And victory share.

KITCHENER

THIS is the man who, sole in Britain, sole
In Europe, by profounder instinct, knew
The strength of Britain ; and that strength he
   drew
Slow into act, upshouldering the whole
Vast weight of effort.   Eyes full on the goal
Saw nothing less ; he held his single clue,
Heedless of obstacle ; intent to do
His one task forthright with unshaken soul.

This is the man whom, dead, the meanest match
With their own stature ; give tongue, and grow
   brave
On the imperfection fools have wit to espy.
His silence towers the grander for their cry,
Troubling his fame no more than yelp and
   scratch
Of jackal could disturb that ocean-grave.

THE TEST

NAKED reality, and menace near
As fire to scorching flesh, shall not affright
The spirit that sees, with danger-sharpened
    sight,
What it must save or die for ; not the mere
Name, but the thing, now doubly, trebly dear,
Freedom ; the breath those hands would choke ;
    the light
They would put out ; the clean air they would
    blight,
Making earth rank with hate, and greed, and
    fear.

Now no man's loss is private : all share all.
Oh, each of us a soldier stands to-day,
Put to the proof and summoned to the call ;
One will, one faith, one peril. Hearts, be high,
Most in the hour that's darkest ! Come what
    may,
The soul in us is found, and shall not die.

YPRES

SHE was a city of patience ; of proud name,
Dimmed by neglecting Time ; of beauty and
   loss ;
Of acquiescence in the creeping moss.
But on a sudden fierce destruction came
Tigerishly pouncing : thunderbolt and flame
Showered on her streets, to shatter them and
   toss
Her ancient towers to ashes. Riven across,
She rose, dead, into never-dying fame.

White against heavens of storm, a ghost, she is
   known
To the world's ends. The myriads of the brave
Sleep round her. Desolately glorified,
She, moon-like, draws her own far-moving tide
Of sorrow and memory ; toward her, each alone,
Glide the dark Dreams that seek an English
   grave.

INTO PEACE

THE ARRAS ROAD

I

THE early night falls on the plain
In cloud and desolating rain.
I see no more, but feel around
The ruined earth, the wounded ground.

There in the dark, on either side
The road, are all the brave who died.
I think not on the battles won ;
I think on those whose day is done.

Heaped mud, blear pools, old rusted wire,
Cover their youth and young desire.
Near me they sleep, and they to me
Are dearer than their victory.

II

Where now are they who once had peace
Here, and the fruitful tilth's increase ?
Shattered is all their hands had made,
And the orchards where their children played.

But night, that brings the darkness, brings
The heart back to its dearest things.
I feel old footsteps plodding slow
On ways that they were used to know.

And from my own land, past the strait,
From homes that no more news await,
Absenting thoughts come hither flying
To the unknown earth where Love is lying.

There are no stars to-night, but who
Knows what far eyes of lovers true
In star-like vigil, each alone
Are watching now above their own ?

III

England and France unconscious tryst
Keep in this void of shadowy mist
By phantom Vimy, and mounds that tell
Of ghostliness that was Gavrelle.

The rain comes wildly down to drench
Disfeatured ridge, deserted trench.
Guns in the night, far, far away,
Thud on the front beyond Cambrai.

But here the night is holy, and here
I will remember, and draw near,
And for a space, till night be sped,
Be with the beauty of the dead.

CAMBRAI

THE silence is a thing to feel and fear ;
It is so human that it hurts the mind
With all that is not, and that was, behind
These gaping walls, this murdered blankness.
  Here
To have had pity on the prisoner
Was penal ; and like engines set to grind
Spirit from flesh, the oppressors toiled to find
Weakness, rejoiced if they could wring a tear.

The houses seem to bleed round the great square,
The silence is so living and intense.
Yet what moves most my heart ? Not the dead
  stare
Of Hate, full-glutted in its hideous will :
It is the thought of Hate's dull impotence,
It is the glory of all it cannot kill.

AN INCIDENT AT CAMBRAI

IN a by-street, blocked with rubble
And any-way tumbled stones,
Between the upstanding house-fronts'
Naked and scorched bones,

Chinese workmen were clearing
The ruins, dusty and arid.
Dust whitened the motley coats,
Where each his burden carried.

Silent they glided, all
Save one, who passed me by
With berry-brown high-boned cheeks
And strange Eastern eye.

And he sang in his outland tongue
Among those ruins drear
A high, sad, half-choked ditty
That no one heeded to hear.

AN INCIDENT AT CAMBRAI

Was it love, was it grief, that made
For long-dead lips that song ?
The desolation of Han,
Or the Never-Ending Wrong ?

The Rising Sun and the Setting,
They have seen this all as a scroll,
Blood-smeared, that the endless years
For the fame of men unroll.

It was come from the ends of the earth
And of Time in his ruin gray,
That song,—the one human sound
In the silence of Cambrai.

OCTOBER, 1918.

THE UNRETURNING SPRING

A LEAF on the gray sand-path
Fallen, and fair with rime !
A yellow leaf, a scarlet leaf,
And a green leaf ere its time.

Days rolled in blood, days torn,
Days innocent, days burnt black,
What is it the wind is sighing
As the leaves float, swift or slack ?

The year's pale spectre is crying
For beauty invisibly shed,
For the things that never were told
And were killed in the minds of the dead.

A DEDICATION

THE thousands of the brave, the happy young,
Our loves and lovers, fallen in France, have
    shrined
That earth for us, and France's name comes
    kind
On English lips. But you, her children, sprung
From the old liberal soil, so rudely wrung,
Out of our own hard pain have we divined
Your harder pain ; hurt body and tortured
    mind,
Where those polluting claws have torn and
    clung.

France, dear to men that honour human things,
To have helped or heartened any of these your
    maimed
And homeless, is itself felicity :
It is to know what suffering man can be ;
How great his heart, when fed from splendid
    springs ;
What human virtue has made you loved and
    famed.

AN ANTHEM
OF THE FIVE NATIONS

O GOD, our race of old went forth,
Our seed about the world is sown
From East to West, from South to North ;
But, mother and children, we are one.
Now we have passed the furnace-fire
And seen the souls of men to shine,
Lift up our hearts to thy desire,
Confirm our faltering wills with thine ;
   One faith to keep, one hope to reap,
   One life to share, one death to dare.

Who glories when another cowers
Before him on a bended knee,
His heart has never beat with ours ;
The free alone can lead the free.
To make a world of men that feel
The wrong of each the wrong of all,
And joy of man our Commonweal,—
Behold our great adventure's call !
   From North afar to Southern star,
   For this the dead together bled.

O God of all our children, hew
From us the stone that they shall build
To beauty grander than we knew,
Our effort in their songs fulfilled.
Make strong our hand and heart ! Preserve
The vision and the will that frees
Within our spirits that proudly serve—
The Sister Nations of the Seas :
> One faith to keep, one hope to reap,
> One life to share, one death to dare.

PEACE

I

LOVELY word flying like a bird across the narrow
  seas,
  When winter is over and songs are in the skies,
Peace, with the colour of the dawn upon the
  name of her,
  A music to the ears, a wonder to the eyes ;
Peace, bringing husband back to wife and son
  to mother soon,
  And lover to his love, and friend to friend,
Peace, so long awaited and hardly yet believed
  in,
  The answer of faith, enduring to the end ;
Tears are in our joy, because the heavy night
  is gone from us
And morning brings the prisoner's release.
How shall we sing her beauty and her blessed-
  ness,
  Saying at last to one another, *Peace ?*

M 2

II

Guns that boomed from shore to shore
And smote the heart with distant dread
Speak no more.
The terror that bestrode the air,
That under ocean kept his lair,
Now is fled.

III

I see, as on a misty morn
When a great ship towering glides
To anchor, out of battle borne,
And looms above her dinted sides,—
Burning through the mist at last
The sun flames on her splintered mast
And the torn flag that from it floats,
And cheering from a thousand throats
Bursts from her splendour and her scars,—
So I see our England come,
Come at last from all her wars
Proudly home.

IV

Now let us praise the dead that are with us
    to-day,
  Who fought and fell before the morning
    shone,
Happy and brave, an innumerable company ;
  This day is theirs, the day their deeds have
    won.
Glory to them, and from our hearts a thanks-
    giving
  In humbleness and awe and joy and pride.
We will not say that their place shall know no
    more of them,
  We will not say that they have passed and
    died :
They are the living, they that bought this hour
    for us
  And spilt their blood to make the world
    afresh ;
One with us, one with our children and their
    heritage,
  They live and move, a spirit in the flesh.

V

With innocence of flowers and grass and dew
Earth covers up her shame, her wounds, her rue.
She pardons and remits ; she gives her grace,
Where men had none, and left so foul a trace.
Peace of the earth, peace of the sky, begins
To sweeten and to cleanse our strifes and sins.
The furious thunderings die away and cease.
But what is won, unless the soul win peace ?

VI

Not with folding of the hands,
Not with evening fallen wide
Over waste and weary lands,
Peace is come ; but as a bride.
It is the trumpets of the dawn that ring ;
It is the sunrise that is challenging.

VII

Lovely word, flying like a light across the happy
    Land,
    When the buds break and all the earth is
       changed,
Bringing back the sailor from his watch upon the
       perilled seas,
    Rejoining shores long severed and estranged,
Peace, like the Spring, that makes the torrent
       dance afresh
    And bursts the bough with sap of beauty
       pent,
Flower from our hearts into passionate recovery
    Of all the mind lost in that banishment.
Come to us mighty as a young and glad deliverer
    From wrong's old canker and out-dated lease,
Then will we sing thee in thy triumph and thy
       majesty,
    Then from our throes shall be prepared our
       peace.

NOTE

THANKS are due to the Editors of various periodicals, English and American, for leave to reprint certain poems; to Messrs. Methuen for permission to reprint "Europe 1901" from *The Death of Adam* and to Mr. Heinemann for permission to reprint "Thunder on the Downs" from *Auguries;* also to the British Committee of the French Red Cross for a like permission in respect of "A Dedication," and to The Overseas Club in respect of "An Anthem of the Five Nations," originally written for music by Mr. Nicholas Gatty (musical rights reserved).

The Author and Publisher desire to thank Mr. Strang for allowing them to reproduce the portrait printed as frontispiece to this volume.

PRINTED BY
WILLIAM BRENDON AND SON, LTD,
PLYMOUTH, ENGLAND

Lightning Source UK Ltd.
Milton Keynes UK
UKOW03f0827010415

248919UK00007B/100/P

draw
Groovy

Thaneeya McArdle

IMPACT
CINCINNATI, OHIO
impact-books.com

Contents

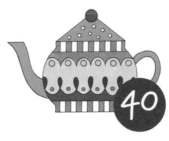

What You Need
drawing paper (any kind works!) • pencil + pencil sharpener
• eraser • markers • colored pencils • crayons •
gel pens • coin or cup to trace circles

This book shows you how to draw fun groovy art that is full of color and style. The best thing about drawing groovy? There are NO RULES! When you draw groovy, you can let your imagination take over and draw the world the way YOU want to see it. Let loose and express yourself!

When you follow these lessons, remember that you *don't* have to copy each step in this book exactly. You can change the colors, choose different shapes and create your own patterns. The possibilities are endless, so you can draw the lessons in this book over and over again, making them different each time. Each drawing can be as unique as you want it to be. Experiment and *have fun*!

Introduction

Drawing Materials

When you follow the lessons in this book, you can use whatever drawing supplies you have on hand. Here are some of the different supplies you can use to create your groovy drawings. Take note of how each type of drawing utensil leaves a different type of mark.

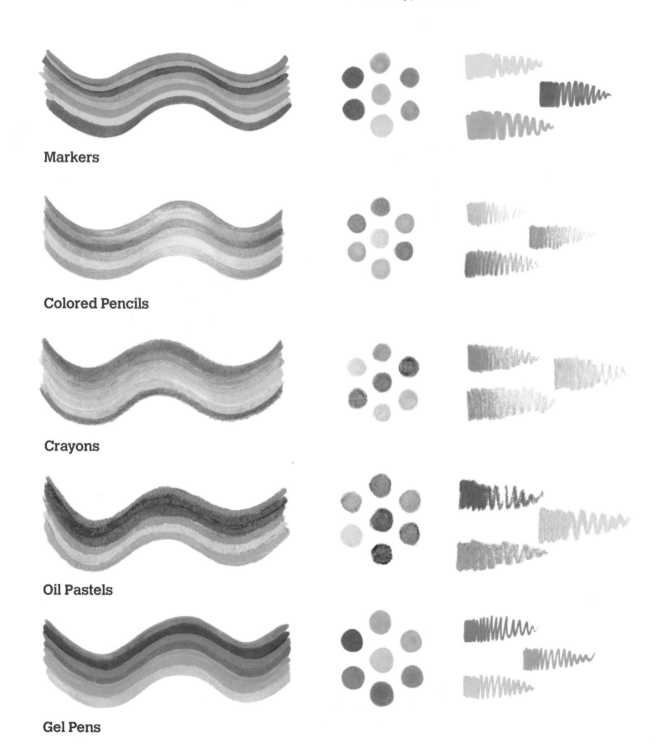

Markers

Colored Pencils

Crayons

Oil Pastels

Gel Pens

Basic Drawing Process

The lessons in this book alternate between two types of drawing processes, drawing with pencil first then coloring, or coloring right from the start. Which way is better? It depends on the lesson and your personal preference. It's really up to you! Sometimes it's easier to draw in pencil first, and sometimes it just adds an extra step you don't really need. Try drawing both ways and see which you prefer.

Black or blue lines in this book always represent pencil marks.

Pencil First Then Coloring

One way to create groovy drawings is to start with a light pencil drawing so you can erase mistakes, then add color with markers, colored pencils or other coloring tools. This process takes a bit more patience, but it helps you learn to plan your drawings, and it all pays off in the end when it's time to color!

Coloring From the Start

You can draw with color right from the start using markers, colored pencils or other coloring tools in your drawing as you go. This process appeals to people who like to jump right in and create art, but the downside is that it can be hard (or impossible) to erase or cover up mistakes when they happen.

Basic Shapes and Patterns

The fun part about drawing groovy is decorating your art with colorful shapes and patterns that fill your art with personality! You can even invent your own patterns by combining basic shapes and patterns.

SHAPES

Circle

Oval

Dot

Spiral

Triangle

Diamond

Star

Half circle

Pointed half circle

Square

Rectangle

Simple flower

Leaf

Pointy leaf

Raindrop

Fat raindrop

Heart

Simple flower

PATTERNS

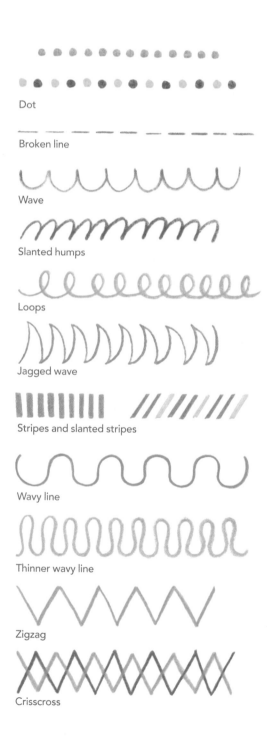

Dot

Broken line

Wave

Slanted humps

Loops

Jagged wave

Stripes and slanted stripes

Wavy line

Thinner wavy line

Zigzag

Crisscross

8

How to Draw a Pattern

A pattern is simply a shape, or a set of shapes, repeated in a row.
Here are several patterns created with multiple shapes.

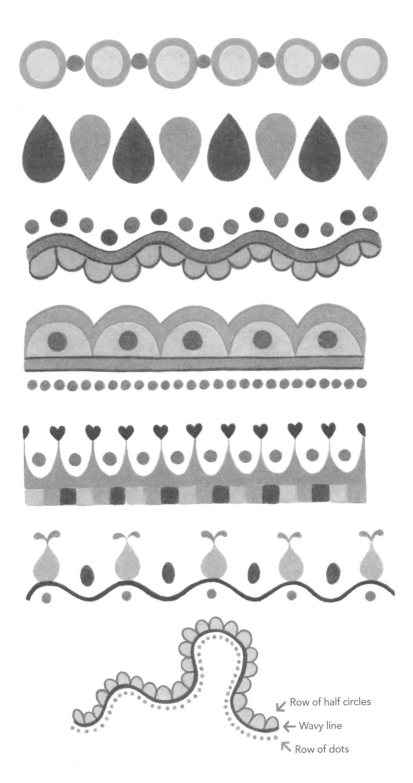

1 A row of circles, big and small.

2 A row of raindrops with every other raindrop drawn upside down.

3 Draw a purple wavy line, then add a row of dots on top and half circles below.

4 Draw a straight pink line and a row of dots underneath. On top of the pink line, draw yellow half circles with blue dots in the center, and then outline the yellow half circles with orange.

5 Now that you know how to draw patterns by repeating shapes, can you see how this pattern is made up of hearts, circles, waves and squares?

6 How many different shapes can you see in this pattern?

7 Patterns don't have to stay in a straight line—they can twist and curve, too!

← Row of half circles
← Wavy line
← Row of dots

Mandalas

Mandalas are fun, abstract designs based on circles, one inside another. Shapes and patterns are added, and the result is like an elegant doodle. Mandalas are created by many different cultures around the world.

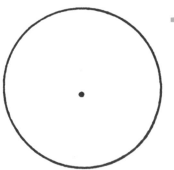

1 Draw a dot with a circle around it. You can also trace a coin, cup or any round object to make a circle.

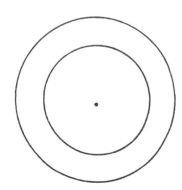

2 Draw another circle around the circle.

3 Add shapes and patterns such as flower petals blooming out of the central dot.

4 Add half-circle petals around the inner circle.

5 Add pointy petals around the outer circle, then add small circles or dots inside each pointy petal.

6 Color it in!

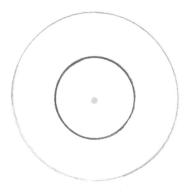

1 Draw a dot, then draw a circle around the dot, and then draw another larger circle around that.

2 Draw a design in the center and color it in.

3 Add patterns around the next circle and color in the background.

4 Draw dots around the outside edge of the circle.

5 Draw petals coming out of each dot.

Marker

Pen

Pen + colored pencil

Marker

Colored pencil

Flowers

Let's draw two different types of pretty flowers. All of the petals give us a chance to use a lot of colors! Once you get the hang of it, you can draw a bunch of flowers to make a garden or draw them inside a pot or vase.

1 Draw a yellow dot.

2 Draw a petal above the dot. Note the shape of the petal.

3 Draw 4 more matching petals around the yellow dot.

4 Draw a small rain-drop shape inside each petal.

5 Draw a pointy petal around each petal.

6 Color the inside shapes.

7 Color the rest of the petals.

8 Add a stem and leaves.

Pen + colored pencil

Colored pencil

1 Draw a circle.

2 Draw 4 short petals around the circle.

3 Draw 4 long petals around each of the short petals.

4 Draw 4 long petals in between the previous petals.

5 Draw 8 petals peeking out between each of the previous long petals.

6 Decorate the petals by adding details such as raindrops.

7 Draw a stem and leaves.

8 Color it in!

Colored pencil

Marker

Butterflies

Butterfly wings are perfect for adding shapes and patterns.
This cute butterfly has pretty wings decorated with flowers. What unique
designs can you come up with?

1 Draw a long oval with a circle on top, then add 2 slightly curved lines for antennae.

2 Draw 2 loops on either side of the butterfly's body. These will be the top set of wings. Try to make them match in shape.

3 Draw the bottom pair of wings.

4 Draw a flower on each wing.

5 Add more shapes to each wing.

6 Color it in!

Pen + colored pencil

Marker

Colored Pencil

Marker

14

1 Draw a long oval and color it in. At the top draw 2 slightly curved lines for antennae.

2 Draw a pair of top wings. Note the shape in the example. Try to make the wings match.

3 Draw a pair of bottom wings. Make them smaller than the top wings. Note the shape in the example.

4 Use different colors to draw shapes inside the wings such as the long raindrop shapes drawn here.

5 Add more shapes such as colored circles. You can also draw stars, hearts, loopy lines or wavy lines, anything you want!

6 Color in the background of the wings.

Pen

Pen + colored pencil

Pen + colored pencil

Marker

Birds

Let's draw a simple bird filled with patterns that give it personality!

1 Starting from the top left of your paper, draw a curvy line that swoops down and then back up like the one you see here.

2 Go back to where you first began and draw a line that swoops up and then down like you see here. This is the bird's body.

3 Draw the bird's tail and 2 curved lines for feet.

4 Draw a line for a beak, a circle for an eye and a curved line for a wing.

5 Add shapes and patterns on the wing and tail.

 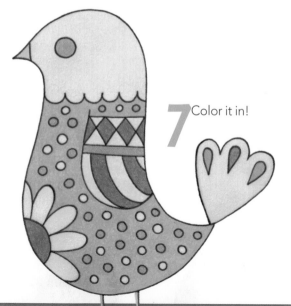

7 Color it in!

6 Decorate the rest of the bird's body with more shapes and patterns.

Marker

Colored pencil

Pen + colored pencil

Marker

17

Owls

Owls are fun to draw because of their wide-open eyes and fabulous feathers.
They look great when you fill them with detail.

1 Draw a gently curving line that goes from left to right at the top of your paper.

2 Below the line, draw 2 large circles in the center that will be the owl's eyes. In between the owl's eyes, draw a V for a beak.

3 Draw a large *U*-shape that curves in slightly on each side near the top, connecting the curved line on top of the owl's eyes.

4 Draw a pair of feet and 2 curved lines for wings.

5 Decorate the eyes and wings with shapes and patterns like dots, flowers and waves.

6 Add more decorations to the owl's body. Let your imagination run wild!

7 Color it in!

Pen

Pen + colored pencil

Pen + colored pencil

Marker

Marker

Marker

19

Owls

Here is another way to draw an owl.
Think of all the designs you can add to its wings, chest and forehead.

1 Draw 2 straight lines that look like a wide V.

2 Draw a pair of eyes with the top of the eyes touching the bottom of the straight lines.

3 Draw a curved *U*-shaped line that goes from the top of one straight line to the top of the other straight line as you see here. This is the owl's body.

4 Draw a curve at the top for the owl's head and 2 curves inside the owl's body to make wings.

5 Draw the owl's feet and a narrow V for a beak.

6 Color in the owl with fun shapes and patterns!

Crayon on colored paper

Pen + colored pencil

Crayon

Marker

Pen + colored pencil

Pen + marker

21

Paisley

Paisley is a cute, fun shape that can be decorated in many ways.
It looks like a raindrop with a little twist at the top.

1 Draw a long, continuous curved line.

2 Without picking up your pencil, bring the curve back up.

3 Curve your line so it connects with the very beginning of your drawing. You've drawn a paisley outline!

4 Begin to decorate the inside of the paisley. Start with a raindrop shape in the big part of the paisley and a circle in the small part.

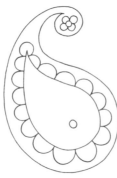

5 Add more patterns and shapes such as flower petals.

6 Draw a line around the outside edge of the paisley's big bulge.

7 Add more detail like lines, stripes, waves, flowers or whatever you can think of.

8 Color it in!

Pen + colored pencil

Pen + colored pencil

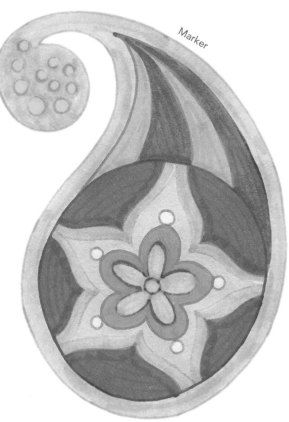

Marker

Pencil

23

Hearts

This cute heart is decorated with colorful shapes and patterns.
Fill it with your own designs to make a fun surprise for someone you love!

1 Draw a heart.

2 Draw a heart around the heart.

3 Draw another heart around the heart.

4 Add decorations around the outside of the heart such as petals, loops, waves and dots.

5 Draw shapes inside the heart such as circles.

6 Add designs to the next layer of the heart.

7 Add more colors and patterns to create a fun, cheerful heart!

Pen + colored pencil

Marker

Pen + colored pencil

25

Shooting Stars

Shooting stars are a bright and colorful way to express your creativity.
Let your inner light shine!

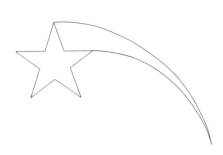

1 Use a pencil to draw a star.

2 Erase the lines inside the star.

3 Draw a small dot to the bottom right of your star. From the top of your star, draw a curved line that swoops down to the dot on the right. Then draw a similar curved line from the right tip of your star to the dot.

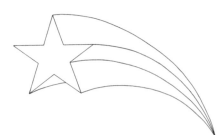

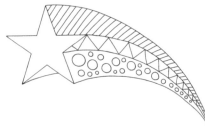

4 Draw more curved lines from the bottom tips of your star to the dot.

5 Draw patterns in between the lines you just drew. You can draw stripes, circles, waves, hearts, anything you want!

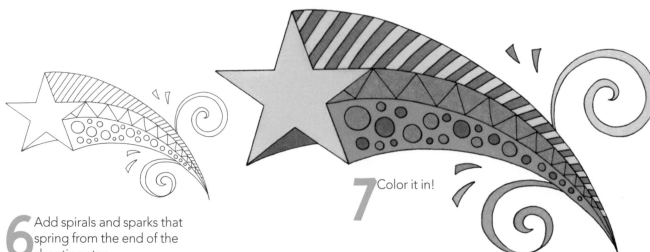

6 Add spirals and sparks that spring from the end of the shooting star.

7 Color it in!

Pen + colored pencil

Pen + colored pencil

Pen + marker

Pen + marker

27

Peace Signs

It's time to promote world peace! This groovy peace sign is full of flowers and smiles.
The steps drawn in blue should be drawn in pencil so you can erase them later.

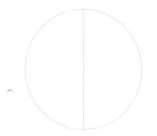

1 Draw or trace a circle. Use a can, cup or any round object to make it perfectly round. Draw a vertical line in the middle of the circle.

2 Starting in the middle of the vertical line, draw a line that goes from the middle to the lower left side of the circle, then do the same thing on the right. This is how you draw a basic peace sign! Now we'll get even more groovy.

3 Draw a circle around the peace sign.

4 Inside the peace sign, draw 4 shapes that echo the shapes of the peace sign. For example, the bottom shapes will look like pie slices. Study the example to see the shapes.

5 Erase the lines you drew in steps 1 and 2. You will be left with the outline of a peace sign that is perfect for coloring and decorating!

6 In the center of the peace sign draw a smiley face. At each point where a straight line touches the circle, draw a flower.

7 Draw circles and flowers (or any other shapes and patterns) to fill in the rest of the peace sign.

8 Color it in!

Colored pencil

Pen + marker

Marker

Marker

29

Toadstools

A toadstool is a mushroom that is often associated with fairies and fairy tales. Draw a colorful mushroom that will attract a ring of dancing fairies!

1 Draw a long line that loops down and back up again. This is the stem or stalk of the toadstool.

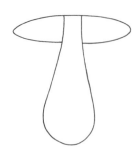

2 Draw a long oval with the top of the oval touching the top of the lines you drew in step 1. This is the inside of the toadstool.

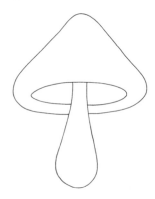

3 Starting below the oval, draw a bigger line that looks like a triangle with rounded edges. This part of the toadstool is called the *cap*.

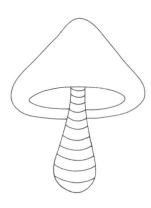

4 Add designs to the stem such as stripes, waves, loops and dots.

5 Add shapes and patterns to the outside of the toadstool. You can draw a bunch of flowers or circles, or you can do rows of different patterns as shown here.

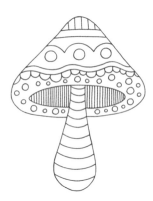

6 Draw vertical lines inside the toadstool. These are called the *gills*.

7 Color it in!

Colored pencil

Pen + colored pencil

Pen + marker

Marker

31

Russian Dolls

Russian nesting dolls usually come in a set of 5 or 6 hollow dolls, each one smaller than the next so they can be stacked inside each other. The dolls are decorated with pretty designs and patterns.

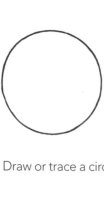

1 Draw or trace a circle.

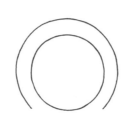

2 Draw a circle around the first circle, but leave the bottom open.

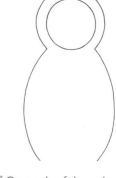

3 On each of the edges of the outer circle, draw long, downward lines that curve outward and back in again.

4 Connect the 2 bottom points by drawing a long oval from point to point.

5 Draw the doll's face. Add hair, eyes and a mouth.

6 Draw patterns on the doll's body. In the center of the doll you can draw a mandala, a flower, a peace sign, a heart or anything you want!

7 Color it in!

Colored pencil

Pen + marker

Marker

Colored pencil

Baby Elephants

Elephants are fun to draw, with their big ears and tummies. Baby elephants don't yet have tusks, so they are easier to draw than grown-up elephants.

1 Start by drawing a long, gently sloping line. This will be the elephant's trunk.

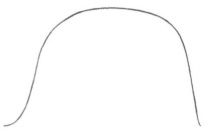

2 From the top of the line draw a hump for the elephant's back. Slope the line downward to create the elephant's back leg.

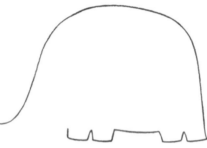

3 Draw 2 back feet, then the elephant's belly, then 2 front feet.

4 Draw the rest of the elephant's front leg and trunk.

5 Draw a circle for the eye, a curved line for the ear, and a tail. Decorate the ear and tail with shapes and colors.

6 Decorate the rest of the elephant's body with shapes such as stripes, circles, flowers, hearts, waves or anything you want! Color it in any way you like!

Pen + colored pencil

Marker

Pen + colored pencil

Colored pencil

35

Cat Heads

Cats are clever, mysterious creatures. Do you ever look in their eyes and wonder what they're thinking? Draw a cat whose fur reflects her personality!

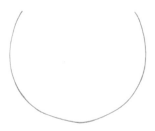

1 Draw a wide *U*-shape with a slight point at the middle bottom.

2 Draw lines to complete each ear and connect the top of the head.

3 Draw triangles inside the cat's ears. Draw a nose and whiskers.

4 Draw the outlines of the cat's eyes.

5 Draw rounded slits for the cat's pupils. You can add little circles to look like reflections of light.

6 Color in the eyes.

7 Decorate the cat's head with shapes and patterns such as mandalas, hearts, dots and paisleys.

Pen + colored pencil

Pen

Pen + marker

Marker

37

Cat Bodies

Complete your cat by drawing its body.
Did you know that when a cat points her tail straight up in the air, she's saying hello?

1 Starting near the end of its left whiskers, draw a line underneath the cat's head that goes down and curves up to form a leg, and then down again and up to form another leg. Study the lines in the example image.

2 Draw a slightly sloping horizontal line from the edge of the cat's head, level with the top of its nose. Draw a similar line extending from the cat's front leg as shown in the example.

3 Draw the cat's tail.

4 Draw the cat's back legs.

5 Add patterns and shapes to the cat's body such as flowers, dots, waves and loops. Color it in!

Pen + marker

Marker

Pen + marker

39

Teapots

If you like tea parties, you'll enjoy drawing your own whimsical teapots!
You can draw them in all shapes and sizes—big and tall or short and small.

1 Draw 2 gently curved lines facing each other.

2 Draw the top and bottom of the teapot using vertical and horizontal lines as shown in the example.

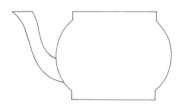

3 Draw the spout of the teapot.

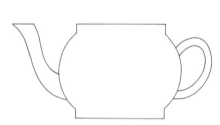

4 Draw the handle of the teapot.

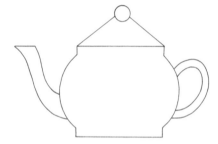

5 Draw the lid of the teapot. In this teapot, the lid looks like a triangle with a circle at the top.

6 Add designs to the teapot such as stripes, loops and dots.

7 Color it in!

Marker

Pen + colored pencil

Pen + colored pencil

Marker

Teacups

Teacups come in many shapes and sizes. Let's draw a tall, elegant teacup and a round teacup decorated with pretty patterns.

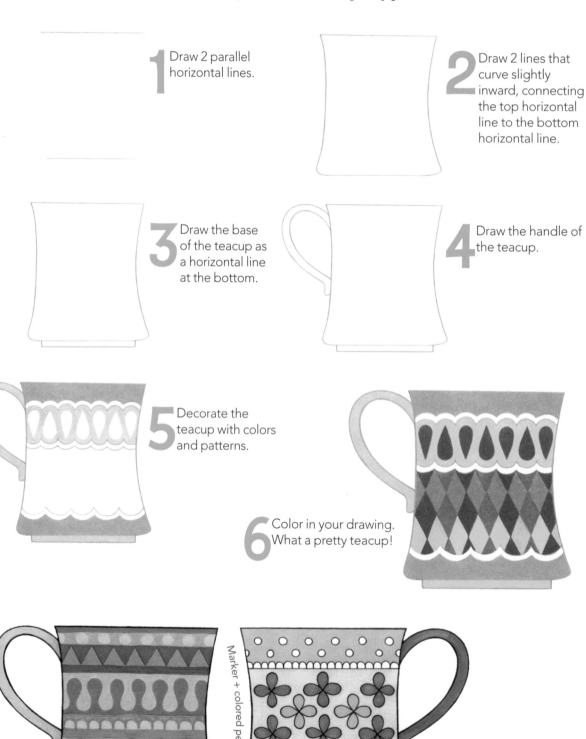

1 Draw 2 parallel horizontal lines.

2 Draw 2 lines that curve slightly inward, connecting the top horizontal line to the bottom horizontal line.

3 Draw the base of the teacup as a horizontal line at the bottom.

4 Draw the handle of the teacup.

5 Decorate the teacup with colors and patterns.

6 Color in your drawing. What a pretty teacup!

Marker + colored pencil

42

1 Draw a long, skinny, horizontal oval.

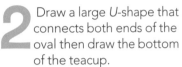

2 Draw a large *U*-shape that connects both ends of the oval then draw the bottom of the teacup.

3 Draw the curvy handle of the teacup.

4 Decorate your teacup with pretty designs.

5 Add more designs to make your teacup unique.

To shade the inside of the teacup, make it darker toward the left and right edges. You can layer colors such as blue and lavender as shown here.

6 Color it in!

Marker

Colored pencil, pen + marker

43

Fancy Hats

Draw a fancy hat to wear to your tea party! You can be as creative as you like and add flowers, stars and other whimsical designs to your hat.

1 Draw a horizontal oval.

2 Starting at the left and right edges of your oval, draw 2 long, gently curving lines downward, and then connect them at the bottom with a wide *U*-shape.

3 Draw the brim of the hat with the left and right sides curved upward.

4 Make your hat special by adding decorations such as flowers or stripes.

5 Add more decorations such as waves, raindrops, hearts and circles.

6 Add decorations to the brim of the hat.

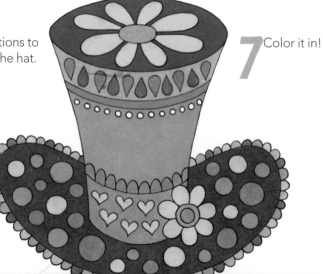

7 Color it in!

Marker

Colored pencil

Marker + pen

45

Hot Air Balloons

The decorations on hot air balloons can be full of color and whimsy.
Draw and decorate a hot air balloon with your own unique designs.

  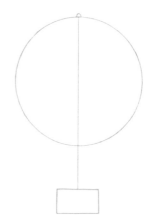

1 Draw a large circle with a very small upside-down U at the top center of the circle. This is the balloon.

2 Draw a rectangle underneath the circle. This is the basket.

3 Draw a straight vertical line from the top center of the circle to the top of the rectangle. This is one of the ropes that connect the balloon to the basket.

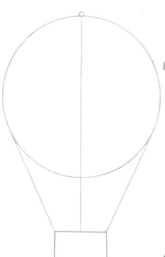

4 Draw straight lines from the sides of the balloon to the top left and right corners of the rectangle.

5 Draw 2 lines that start from the top center of the balloon and curve gently downward, ending on top of the basket.

6 Now that you've drawn the balloon, basket and ropes, it's time to decorate your balloon with fun shapes and patterns!

7 Draw things like hearts, waves, circles, stars, stripes and anything else you can think of. Don't forget to decorate and color the basket!

Crayon + marker

Marker

Marker

47

Smiling Sun

This smiling sun has big eyes and groovy rays.
By doing some light shading around the edge of your sun, you can make it look 3-dimensional.

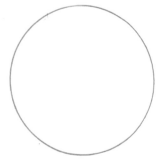

1 Draw a large circle. You can trace a cup, glass, lid, coaster or other round object.

2 Give your sun a face by drawing a pair of eyes, a curved line for a smile and 2 small circles at the edges of the smile to create rosy cheeks.

3 Color in the eyes and cheeks.

4 Color the sun yellow with orange shading around the edge of the circle.

5 Draw a ring of small petal shapes around the outside of the circle.

6 Draw the rays of the sun. You can draw the rays as lines, spikes, triangles or pointy waves as shown here.

Colored pencil

Marker

Marker

Pen + marker

49

Mandala Flowers With Leaves

It's easy to turn mandalas (see page 10) into flowers. All you have to do is add a stem and leaves. Here's two ways to draw stems and cute leaves.

1 Draw a mandala and color it in.

2 At the bottom of the mandala, draw lines that curve gently downward to make a stem.

3 Draw a leaf. Repeat the same shape inside the leaf but smaller.

4 Draw a similar leaf on the opposite side of the stem.

5 Color it in using 2 different shades of green.

Alternate leaf colorings

1 Draw a mandala.

2 Starting at the bottom of the mandala, draw a long, straight green line going downward.

3 At the top of the green line, draw a green sideways raindrop shape on either side of the line with the points touching.

4 Draw another pair of raindrop shapes below your first pair.

5 Draw more pairs of leaves until you reach the bottom of the stem.

You can also add leaves to your mandala flowers by leaving out the stem and drawing the leaves directly touching the flower.

Flowers in Vases

Now that you know how to draw flowers and leaves, you can also draw pretty vases to put them in. Your vases can be tall and narrow or wide and bulky. It's up to you!

1 Near the middle of your paper, draw a short horizontal line. Near the bottom of your paper draw another horizontal line, a bit longer this time. Make sure to leave enough blank space at the top of your paper to draw flowers.

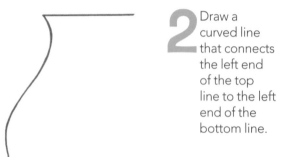

2 Draw a curved line that connects the left end of the top line to the left end of the bottom line.

3 Connect the right ends of the lines by drawing a line that mirrors the curved line you drew in step 2.

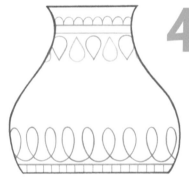

4 Decorate your vase with patterns and shapes like hearts, stars, waves, dots, stripes and anything else you can think of.

5 Color it in!

6 Add flowers and leaves.

Colored pencil

Pen + colored pencil

Pen + colored pencil

Pen + marker

53

Vines

If you like to doodle, you'll love drawing swirly vines. They're fun to draw on the edges of your notebook paper, or you can cover an entire sheet of paper with them.

1 Draw an elegant line with swirls and loops.

2 Draw lines that run parallel to the swirls and loops.

3 Color in the swirls and loops.

4 Draw patterns around the outside of the swirls and loops such as circles, petals and waves.

5 Add decorations such as dots, raindrops and small swirls.

6 Finish the vine by drawing flowers at each end. Color away!

Colored pencil + pen

Colored pencil

Marker + pen

Squiggle Abstracts

Abstract art is fun to create because you don't have to worry about making the art look like anything real. Instead, you focus on drawing shapes and patterns using any colors you want. Let the colors and patterns dance across your paper!

1 Draw a loopy squiggly line that overlaps itself in several places. Overlapping is important because it creates closed-in areas that you'll be decorating in the next steps.

2 Start drawing decorations on the outside and the inside of your loopy line.

3 Move from section to section drawing patterns inside the closed areas as well as outside the lines.

4 Draw things like dots, hearts, stripes, swirls, raindrops, waves, loops and flowers.

5 Experiment with different colors and shapes.

6 Continue adding decorations to your drawing. Try to make it feel balanced.

7 You are finished when you feel you are finished. There is no right or wrong when it comes to drawing squiggle abstracts!

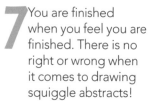

Colored pencil + pen

Pen

Marker

Mehendi

Mehendi refers to detailed decorations that are drawn on people's hands in India and other countries. Instead of drawing on your own hand, we'll draw mehendi-style designs on paper. Traditionally mehendi is drawn in one color, but you can use many different colors to express who you are!

1 Trace your hand onto a sheet of paper. Be sure to trace your wrist too.

2 In the center of the hand, draw a mandala or a flower or a heart or a star or any other image that you feel represents who you are.

3 Draw shapes and patterns on the fingers. Invent your own patterns by combining shapes like circles and raindrops as shown in this example.

4 Draw a pattern across the wrist.

5 Color it in!

Colored pencil

Marker

Colored pencil

59

Toadstool Houses

Earlier you learned to draw groovy toadstools.
Now let's turn those toadstools into colorful houses—the perfect homes for tiny gnomes!

1 On the bottom half of your paper draw a curved line that will be the stalk. This will be the first floor of the house.

2 On top of the stalk draw the cap of the toadstool, which looks like a triangle with very rounded corners. This will be the roof and the top story of the house.

3 Draw a chimney on the cap and a front door on the stalk.

4 Draw windows on the cap.

5 Decorate the cap and the stalk with shapes and patterns. Add grass.

6 Color it in! You can also draw flowers and butterflies if you like.

Marker

Marker + pen

Colored pencil + pen

61

Bonus Art

Now that you know how to turn a simple line drawing into a groovy masterpiece, you can add colorful shapes and patterns to any drawing such as this funky sheep, sugar skull and pretty peacock!